dream gardens
of England

100 inspirational gardens

dream gardens
of England

Barbara Baker

Jerry Harpur and Marcus Harpur

MERRELL
LONDON · NEW YORK

You dreamed us, and we made your dream come true.
We are your vision, here made manifest.
You sowed us, and obediently we grew,
But, sowing us, you sowed more than you knew
And something not ourselves has done the rest.

So wrote Vita Sackville-West in her poem 'The Garden' (1946). For centuries gardens have fulfilled, and sometimes exceeded, the dreams of their makers. This book captures the essence of 100 dream gardens in photographs and words, with the aim of inspiring the reader. The gardens range from Yorkshire to Cornwall, and in size from 5.5 by 6 metres (Kensington Road, Bristol; 56) to 405 hectares (Hatfield House, Hertfordshire; 9). They include both public and private gardens, in virtually every style, taking the reader on a varied journey of discovery.

Typical English gardens tend to reflect the formality of Tudor times, pastoral preoccupations in the landscape era, the evocative idealism of cottage gardens, vibrant Victorian bedding, Arts and Crafts exuberance enclosed in restraint, naturalism and the minimal. Large country-house gardens sometimes combine several of these elements in a formal area around the house, perhaps with an ornamental parterre, herbaceous walks leading to more informal areas and parkland beyond. But the gardens within these pages are exceptional: rules are broken, originality creeps in, influences from abroad and climate change add new dimensions, and, most significantly, individual visions are pursued.

Gardens reflect the character of their makers, but these gardens are not confined to famous designers – although such innovators as William Kent, Lancelot 'Capability' Brown, Gertrude Jekyll, Vita Sackville-West and Christopher Bradley-Hole are included – because dreams are universal. When a garden is created by its owner it acquires a unique personality: romanticism combined with serenity in the Kitchen Garden (7); grandeur at Helmingham Hall (27); exuberance in the Magic Garden (30); elegance at Broughton Castle (37); confidence at Ousden House (41); attention to detail at the Old Rectory, Norfolk (53); and eccentricity at Barnards Farm (68) – these are just some examples. Additionally, and importantly, owner-designed gardens have the chance to develop and evolve. Gardening never ends, and to achieve success one must constantly re-evaluate, take risks and boldly be prepared to change. After all, dreams can be about the future as well as the past.

So what is a dream garden? For the owner, it is the realization of their vision and aspirations. To the visitor, it can instil a feeling of joy, evoke memories or

Broughton Castle, Oxfordshire (37)

be thought-provoking. The best dream gardens combine all of these. There is a heightened atmosphere where the ordinary is rarefied and refined, and sensations are not quite of the waking world. Garsington Manor (2), Blakenham Woodland Garden (24), The Old Zoo (44), Rousham (50) and Beckley Park (86) are just a few, particularly clear, instances. Anything is possible in a dream, as in a garden.

Amazingly, most of the gardens in this book originated from nothing: brambles and nettles were conquered and sometimes the very lie of the land was transformed. Gardening is an art form, dependent on good craftsmanship. Whatever the size or style, dream gardens display keen attention to colour combinations, texture and form, light and shade, void and mass, structure and softness. Some include such features as water and sculpture; some rely on tradition, others on idiosyncrasy; all require knowledge of plants. They are a labour of love yet appear effortless. But above all, perhaps, what unites all these gardens is the passion, dedication and enthusiasm with which they were made and are maintained. They are not showcases, experiments or museums, but an expression of their creators' dreams: places that their owners enjoy looking at and being in daily.

In England, over the last few years, there has been a huge increase in interest not only in gardening, but also in garden visiting, for gardens should ideally be shared. The National Gardens Scheme, where gardens — particularly private ones — open to the public in return for a donation to charity, is enormously beneficial. Many of the gardens in this book, although normally private, do open occasionally. The listing at the back will help readers in this regard. But this book is intended for armchair browsers as well as those inspired to visit in person; both can 'borrow' ideas depicted here. Like people we admire, gardens or plant combinations may be emulated and our knowledge enriched.

Having always enjoyed visiting gardens myself, meeting passionate people and trying to encapsulate experience in words, I have found great pleasure in writing this book. I am very grateful to all the gardeners who gave their time so generously. I hope that all who read the book and see its wonderful photographs will be encouraged to fulfil their own dreams, or be inspired to create new ones. I started with a quotation from a poem by Vita Sackville-West, who created one of the most influential gardens of all time, on a grand scale. I would like to end with words from the website of the smallest garden in the National Gardens Scheme, 28 Kensington Road in Bristol, owned by Grenville Johnson and Alan Elms: 'We feel that gardens, irrespective of their size, have the capability of raising the spirits and feeding the imagination and soul.'

Kensington Road, Bristol (56)

I

Little Larford

ASTLEY BURF, WORCESTERSHIRE

This terraced garden on a hillside around a picturesque cottage is resplendent with colour. Derek Walker, who lives here with his wife, has been in the gardening trade since he was seventeen, owning garden centres and a nursery that supplied local authorities with plants. His great love of tulips and bedding is an obvious result, but he also has a weakness for lilies, which he grows in pots to be plunged into the garden wherever space occurs. Another enthusiasm is for exhibition vegetables, which are not hidden in a corner of the garden but proudly displayed in wood-and-mesh huts. Robinson's mammoth onions, leeks wound in plastic sheets, potatoes in barrels and carrots in a straight core of 'magic mix' drilled in sand are all grown for perfect shape and size. But the real showstoppers are the dazzling displays of tulips in spring, giving way to bedding in summer. Every year three-quarters of the planting is replaced; moreover, everything is immaculate. It is a great achievement.

RIGHT, TOP
Although the Walkers have lived at Little Larford only since 2003, they saw its potential straight away. In spring, ambitious displays of tulips are seen with yellow *Euonymus fortunei* 'Emerald 'n' Gold'.

RIGHT, BOTTOM
Quantities of containers provide additional colour. The 1.2 hectares (3 acres) of natural woodland behind the house are a bird sanctuary.

OPPOSITE
Although the central oak tree was already there, paving was added and 400 tons of sand replaced with topsoil. Shrubs and perennials were planted for continuous interest, but each year 20,000 tulips of about 140 varieties are planted in swirls and blocks.

OVERLEAF
A small wooden gazebo is almost submerged among shrubs and summer bedding: a kaleidoscope of colour framed by a laurel hedge.

2

Garsington Manor

OXFORDSHIRE

There is something for everyone at dreamy
Garsington. The Tudor manor has drawn
innumerable literary luminaries, and the
garden – largely created by Lady Ottoline and
Philip Morrell in the 1920s – is gorgeous.
There are three distinct areas: an Italianate
pool with statues set against tall yew hedges;
a wild garden with stream and pond; and a
box parterre divided into twenty-four squares,
with a clipped Irish yew cone at each corner.
In spring the squares are filled with tulips,
like jewels in the compartments of a casket.
Garsington is also home to an annual season
of operas staged in a courtyard behind
the parterre. Performances extend into the
garden: in one, a shepherdess ran through
with two lambs, and – magical and very
funny – the spies of Alexander the Great
hid in mock yew cones that moved.

RIGHT
This loggia with dry-stone terrace
was designed by the Morrells
(influenced by their travels in Italy)
and architect Philip Tilden. It forms
a natural stage for opera, which
has been performed at Garsington
since 1982. The gardens provide
an exceptional setting, as Virginia
Woolf had recognized when she
wrote: 'Is the air ever normal at
Garsington? No, I think even the sky
is done up in pale yellow silk.'

PAGE 20, TOP
The manor, built by William
Wickham, is seen from the elegant
Italianate pool. Yew hedging adds
formality and height, and creates
contrasts of light and shade.

PAGE 20, BOTTOM
The fabulous parterre holds tulips
and forget-me-nots, punctured by
rapier Irish yews.

PAGE 21, TOP
In the cool woodland garden, the
burgeoning leaves of beech contrast
with darker green fastigiate yews.

PAGE 21, BOTTOM
A bridge leads to a small island at
the centre of the pond, surrounded
by a froth of cow parsley.

3

Fawler Copse

KINGSTON LISLE, OXFORDSHIRE

This garden by renowned landscape designer
Christopher Bradley-Hole merges seamlessly
with the unique house, built of green oak and
glass, designed by Roderick James Architects
in 1998. Both produce an atmosphere of
rhythm and space, drama and minimalism
combined. 'I thought it was very important
to create a formal courtyard at the point of
arrival in front,' explains Bradley-Hole, 'so
I created a square, but with a curved wall at
the side of the house, which relates to the
landscape, and a radius line that related to
a return angle in the house. The back of
the house goes in and out, and there is open
country beyond, so I felt any intervention
between the two should not be fussy, but
bold and simple. I had a big oak deck with a
consistent line.' Squares and rectangles cut out
of the wood are filled with flowing grasses.
From low mounds to wafting plumes and
finally seed heads, they perform spectacularly
all year. Two more cut-out elements complete
the deck: a fire pit and a water feature.

RIGHT
The original owners had five young
children, 'terrors', who tricycled
straight into the planting, so Bradley-
Hole deliberately chose plants that
related to the landscape but were
also fairly tough: *Miscanthus sinensis*
'Gracillimus', *Calamagrostis* × *acutiflora*,
sedum and *Persicaria amplexicaulis*.

OPPOSITE, TOP
The timber-framed house, which
has faded to silver, has slatted areas
painted blue, giving a seaside feel
that is reinforced by stilt-supported
balconies at the rear. Round the edge
of the terrace, slab paving and tiny
pebbles (the beach theme again)
merge with an undulating lawn that
disappears into open countryside.

OPPOSITE, BOTTOM
The oak screen at the side of
the house formalizes some of the
fencing seen in distant fields. At
the bottom of the screen, etched
glass affords a silhouetted view of
the ornamental grasses.

4

Pitts Deep Cottage

LYMINGTON, HAMPSHIRE

Silvery grey permeates here, in the sea, rocks, weathered timber, foliage and found objects. Susan Campbell's house is embraced by her garden, which terminates at the front in large rocks from Lyme Regis – a barrage against the sea, with its constant, eroding lapping. Beyond is a fabulous view of the Solent and the Isle of Wight. Silver-leaved *Halimium atriplicifolium* acts as a windbreak against the buffeting conditions, while the frothy flowers of tamarisk remind Susan of sea foam. Much of the planting is inspired by local wild varieties, and includes cardoons, sea kale, chives and succulents. A catenary formed from rope found on the shore is festooned with roses and clematis. A dramatic arch of two fused oak-tree trunks – another found item – leads from the rope garden. *Quercus suber* (cork oak) has grown from an acorn collected on holiday; a myrtle originated from a piece brought back from Osborne House. Everything possible is salvaged, including sculptural driftwood resembling bones. Parallels with Derek Jarman's garden at Dungeness are inevitable, but Susan is quick to point out that her garden preceded his.

RIGHT
Susan Campbell designs kitchen gardens, and indeed has one of her own, as well as an orchard. Against the wall of her office is *Rosa* 'New Dawn'.

OPPOSITE, TOP
A weathered timber deck surrounded by rope makes a perfect place to sit and watch the racing at Cowes. Rocks to the right shield against erosion, while the tamarisk was inspired by visits to Greece, where it is grown as a tree rather than a shrub.

OPPOSITE, BOTTOM
The garden is filled with the treasures of the sea, from dramatic driftwood to glass bottles.

24

OPPOSITE, TOP
A group of oaks provides the ideal spot for a hammock.

OPPOSITE, BOTTOM
The glade has a secluded atmosphere, although the sea is still visible through the tree branches. Crack willows (*Salix fragilis*, which bends, cracks and re-roots) are underplanted with narcissi and colchicum for spring.

RIGHT
To the east, a pond was dug in marshland. The moon, doubled in reflection, perfects this scene, with ash and oak silhouetted on the right and the sea behind.

5

Eastgrove Cottage
SHRAWLEY, WORCESTERSHIRE

Cottage gardens are quintessentially English, and for many (including myself), they fulfil the criteria of a dream garden – informal and nostalgic, packed with flowers. Eastgrove, approached down a narrow rural lane, is a wonderful example, with a bonus: owner Carol Skinner had artist parents, and says that colour is very important to her. Rather than a mix of jarring hues, the hardy borders show subtle, masterful combinations in both flowers and foliage. Structure is created by the strategic use of height and the unusual undulating hedge; as in the half-timbered cottage, there are no straight lines in the garden. An old-fashioned charm presides. Every outbuilding is clad with flowers, as are the pergolas, which lead from one area to the next and out to meadowland and a small arboretum with views of the countryside. Art and nature are skilfully combined, but this billowing garden also has soul.

The garden surrounds a seventeenth-century yeoman farmhouse. Tumbling abundance and a desire for house and garden to be 'all of a piece' are fulfilled. A clipped hedge of shrubby honeysuckle (*Lonicera nitida*), nearly fifty years old, forms a wavy backbone, dividing and hiding different areas. In the centre *Cornus alternifolia* 'Argentea' draws the eye. In the foreground are *Rosa* 'Président de Sèze' and *Penstemon* 'Pennington Gem', with *R.* 'Petite de Hollande'; *R.* 'Tuscany Superb', with its flowers of deepest crimson–purple, is behind the sundial. At the back is *Philadelphus* 'Boule d'Argent'.

OPPOSITE, TOP LEFT
A brick barn is the perfect backdrop for hotter colours. *Achillea* 'Moonshine' and *Libertia peregrinans* mix with English marigolds; behind, *Salvia* × *jamensis* 'Red Velvet' is set off against the copper foliage of *Physocarpus opulifolius* 'Diabolo'.

OPPOSITE, TOP RIGHT
In the Morning Border the yellow buds of low *Anthemis tinctoria* 'E.C. Buxton' and *Santolina pinnata* subsp. *neapolitana* 'Edward Bowles' mingle with Hidcote lavender and the dark spires of *Salvia nemorosa* 'Caradonna'. Behind are *Achillea* 'Coronation Gold' and the tall grass *Elymus magellanicus*.

OPPOSITE, BOTTOM
The tactile, snaking hedge enfolds and unifies this curvaceous garden.

RIGHT
A supremely satisfying patchwork of repeated soft pink, fresh yellow and glaucous green is achieved with dusky Astrantia 'Hadspen Blood', *Hosta sieboldiana* var. *elegans*, *Rosa* 'De Rescht' and *Penstemon* 'Pennington Gem'. Height is provided by *Prunus serrula*, and texture by ferns, bergenia and euphorbia.

6

Painswick Rococo Garden

GLOUCESTERSHIRE

Situated in the Cotswolds, Painswick garden lies in a valley hidden behind the house. On entering, most of the garden is laid out before you, and is a rare example of realism and extreme artifice. Naturalized snowdrops whiten the ground each February, while flamboyant architectural features hark back to a time when the gentry loved pleasure gardens, parties and frivolity. The garden was laid out in the early eighteenth century, and a painting from 1748 has enabled the overgrown jungle that existed in the 1970s to be redeveloped into one of the only Rococo gardens in England. Most striking is the eighteenth-century Exedra (a white-painted, semi-circular colonnade) standing over herbaceous borders. Below is a kitchen garden, where triangular beds are enclosed by espaliered apple and pear trees. Many of the trees bear labels with people's names, presumably those in whose memory they were planted. Eerily, the first I saw was inscribed 'Barbara Baker'.

RIGHT, TOP
The Eagle House, set on a steep bank, gives a bird's-eye view of the garden.

RIGHT, BOTTOM
No one knows how the famous snowdrops first came to Painswick, but James Atkins, a snowdrop grower, did live in one of the estate cottages in the 1860s. His name has since been given to tall, fragrant *Galanthus* 'Atkinsii'.

OPPOSITE, TOP
Drifts of *Galanthus nivalis* sparkle under beech trees: joyful harbingers of spring.

OPPOSITE, BOTTOM
In winter the rose walk takes on a cloistered appearance, with its gothic arches and bare branches.

7

The Kitchen Garden

TROSTON, SUFFOLK

This garden (and the cottage too) is what
most young girls dream of owning. It is an
exquisitely romantic blend of Beatrix Potter
and Laura Ashley with an additional feature
of serene elegance: a green corridor at the
centre. This formal yew-lined *allée* is almost
like a hallway in a house, with eight different
rooms leading off it. Nearest the house
are blowsy borders and box balls. Split-
cane cloches surround some plants, to
give protection from the ducks and hens
that roam the garden, which is owned by
journalist Francine Raymond. A large duck
pond – hidden until reached via a meadow
of wild grasses – forms the back boundary
of the garden, with wheatfields beyond.
Francine says: 'I am interested in texture, and
green is my favourite colour. I don't really
like flowers.' Although the first part of
this statement is borne out by her garden,
the second is not. Round a rose screen
is a cutting garden. The vegetable garden,
too, is not devoid of self-seeded flowers,
contributing to the charm, lingering happy
atmosphere and beauty of this garden.

The yard is entered under a willow
arch above a small gate in a low
picket fence. Cloches and pots hold
an attractive array of plants and
vegetables, most of which are for sale.

8

Sleightholmedale Lodge

FADMOOR, NORTH YORKSHIRE

This garden is magnificently positioned on the steep, south-facing slopes of a wooded valley in the Yorkshire Moors. Rosanna James, the third generation of her family to garden here, explains that she has 'mended rather than altered it'. The garden has separate areas of planting for different seasons: a spring garden heartens with *Primula elatior*, thalictrum, polemonium, bulbs and blossom; and the walled garden is a wonderful exuberance of colour in summer. Surprisingly, Mrs James says that she has always been interested in wild flowers, but she never thinks about colour at all. 'My only interest is whether the plant will survive in the proposed place.' A favourite is meconopsis, and several hundred blue, pink, yellow and red specimens thrive here. Mrs James also likes long grass and meadow planting as a background for herbaceous plants, and used it to great effect before it became fashionable. Additionally, she has created an orchard, with both bulbs and hardy geraniums naturalized in grass. Unconventionality and unpretentiousness result in a flourishing feast of colour descending into the landscape.

9

Hatfield House

HERTFORDSHIRE

Hatfield House and its gardens are steeped in history, and it is this sense that envelops the visitor, for the gardens have been remade as they might have been, in sympathy with the house, built by Robert Cecil in 1611. The gardens, originally planted by John Tradescant the Elder, comprise several different areas, all now run organically. Seen from above, a knot garden impresses with its perfect box patterns and central golden cherub fountain, glinting grandly. A lime walk provides dappled shade, which would have been especially appreciated by the eighteenth-century ladies of the house. It leads to a privy garden, where more exuberant planting in pink, mauve and blue conveys a personal, plantsman's touch (that of the Dowager Lady Salisbury). There is a scented garden, a herb garden and a holly walk, where the dark, textured sides complement the carpet of lawn between. The wilderness garden, with its long grasses and flowing wild flowers, provides a welcome contrast to the largely formal areas surrounding the house and the 405 hectares (1000 acres) of parkland.

RIGHT
Lions rampant watch over the West Garden and park from the roof of the Jacobean house.

OPPOSITE, TOP
A hexagonal seat offers cold comfort beside a frost-powdered yew hedge.

OPPOSITE, BOTTOM
A silhouetted pergola frames the wintry scene in a composition of contrasts.

OVERLEAF
An icing of frost gives an ethereal quality to the East Garden, which leads down to the lake. This garden was designed to be viewed from above, as here, to appreciate fully the formal parterres, topiary and rectilinear maze.

10

St Helens

STEBBING, ESSEX

In a picturesque village with a bowling green and coloured cottages is St Helens, a small house on the High Street. In 1973, when Joan and Stephen Bazlinton moved in, it was a two-up, two-down with a tiny garden. Now it is surprising to see the extended house, but, in particular, the 0.4-hectare (1-acre) garden, which reveals itself in stages. Weaving paths offering different joys culminate in a huge, wondrously beautiful pond. As if in a painting, the green foreground gives way to soft browny mauve, while stillness and peace envelop you. A woodland area over a bridge is carpeted with ivy and canopied with ash. Leaves become more dramatic in a jungly area, then back towards the house are shrubs, topiary, vegetables and a rainbow iris bed. The Bazlintons are fortunate to have four natural springs in their garden: they modestly believe that they have worked with what they were given, and that their responsibility is one of stewardship and care, as part of a bigger picture of Creation.

RIGHT, TOP
A 'Monet' bridge forms a backdrop to the large leaves of *Rheum palmatum*, a foil to the orange flowers of *Euphorbia griffithii* 'Dixter'.

RIGHT, BOTTOM
Ivy is used extensively as ground cover. Colour is provided here in roses and irises behind and the tiered flowers of *Viburnum plicatum* f. *tomentosum* 'Mariesii' beside the clipped *Taxus baccata*.

OPPOSITE, TOP
A bridge draws you past variegated elder and *Petasites japonicus* (in the foreground). Behind the pond is a huge wave of bamboo (*Fargesia murielae*), which flowered and died, but nevertheless looks stunning. Miraculously, new shoots are appearing.

OPPOSITE, BOTTOM, FROM LEFT
A beech hedge surrounds the small front gate; in front of the summer house, a box parterre incorporates the year 2000 and the Greek letters alpha and omega; a swing hangs from an ash tree by a seat perfect for contemplation.

II

The Old Mill

RAMSBURY, WILTSHIRE

This garden has water as its heart, having
the River Kennet, a millstream and channels
running through it, and the sound of water
is ever present. Also striking is the skilful
combination of the wild and the cultivated.
When the Dallases bought the property in
1995, unusually it was the highly manicured
garden round the house that they disliked
and first changed. Now, although it contains
topiary animals and a herb parterre, the
colour-themed beds hold relaxed planting.
The area across the river was once
impenetrable, but is now 'lived-in', with
little paths leading in different directions,
whether to a football pitch, into an orchard,
or towards a wide gravel path bordered by
hostas and roses. Above all, though, it is the
reflected light from the water and the many
shades of green from the trees that give this
garden a special quality. James Dallas knew
the garden as a child, when a friend lived
there, and he always loved the water. Now
his wife, Annabel, has joined his dream and
helped to realize it, as he acknowledges, in
creating this garden.

A view over the Kennet to the Old
Mill, the oldest parts of which date
back to 1740. In early summer beds
beside the river are fresh with
poppies, nepeta and primulas.

In this garden, a naturalistic look is sometimes achieved by means of the planting medium. Oriental poppies and delphiniums are planted in earth here, but elsewhere verbascum and nigella are grown in gravel to encourage self-seeding. Conversely, some flowers, such as alstroemeria and day lilies, are planted in grass, appearing to have sprung up on their own.

OPPOSITE, TOP
A path leads through informal planting in reds and purples. Impressive obelisks add height, echoing the spires of the delphiniums.

OPPOSITE, BOTTOM
It is possible that Christopher Lloyd's grandfather sat in this garden, with its sheltering yew hedges, when he rented the house as a fishing cottage. The pergola has *Rosa* 'Madame Alfred Carrière' and *Vitis* 'Brant' growing up its wooden posts, with tiarella at the base. It was placed deliberately to follow the lines of the house, as were the paths and hedges on this side of the river.

12

Fernlea Road

BURNHAM-ON-CROUCH, ESSEX

Few gardeners who have created a beautiful oasis from scratch would say, 'I don't like gardening', but this is what Frances Franklin admitted. Nor would one imagine a low-maintenance garden to be filled with floriferous borders, yet Frances and her husband, Andrew, have achieved this 'just by solving problems'. The 15-by-15-metre (49-by-49-ft) garden, in the UK's third-driest area, has a Moroccan feel. There are blue-painted sheds, mosaics, a vine-covered pergola and a tent. With inspiration gleaned from magazines and flower shows, Frances created several features herself, such as the ravishing pond with raised mosaic sides, brimful of still water. Deep blue, pink, purple and bronze dominate the planting schemes in the gravel beds. Pots spill with plants, too, irrigated by an automatic system. When the Franklins moved in there was just parched lawn. They tried to become self-sufficient, but realized they did not enjoy growing vegetables from seed, or watering, preferring to relax with a glass of wine. Now they have three stunning seating areas from which to appreciate the tranquillity of their haven.

RIGHT
Movement, as well as contrasting foliage forms, is important to Frances. She also enjoys tracking down artisans and skilfully placing their work in the garden.

OPPOSITE, TOP
A plastic roof concealed by a vine-covered pergola creates an outdoor room, much used for relaxing, in this garden that the owners insist is low-maintenance.

OPPOSITE, BOTTOM
The blue-tiled pond was an early creation in the garden, initiating the Moroccan feel.

13

Petworth

WEST SUSSEX

When people consider English gardens, they tend to think either of cottage gardens or of landscape gardens, and Petworth is a prime example of the latter. The majestic deer park covers 283 hectares (700 acres) and was designed by Lancelot 'Capability' Brown between 1751 and 1764. Walking there, one might almost imagine one was in natural countryside, except that everything is perfect – altered by Brown to make it so. The composition of clumps of trees, water and undulating grassland was all-important when combining art with nature, and the scale of work to achieve these effects was often huge. At Petworth a serpentine lake was created by damming a series of small ponds, and laying 17,000 tons of clay over the sandy surface. A further 47,000 tons of soil was used to fill the natural valley below. The resulting view inspired many of Turner's most idyllic landscapes and remains a joy today.

'Capability' Brown was so named because of his accomplishment in bringing out the 'capabilities' of an area for landscaping. Here, a gentle hill above the lake is clothed in gold by naturalized narcissi. A temple among groups of trees draws the eye and enhances the view.

14

The Old Rectory
SUDBOROUGH, NORTHAMPTONSHIRE

This irresistible country garden in an attractive village has sweeping lawns and colour-themed beds, leading to a pond and brook. Anne and Anthony Huntington have lived here since 1984, when they fell in love with the house. Anne claims: 'Nothing about me is informal, so my garden isn't either.' Yet everything is pretty as well as artistic, with an elegant balance between effervescent planting, restraining box and naturalized bulbs. Anne loves the variety here, but has a passion for her large collection of nodding hellebores in spring. In summer peonies are prized, both blowsy herbaceous and voluptuous, tissue-paper-flowered tree peonies. Rupert Golby advised on planting the borders, and renowned writer and designer Rosemary Verey designed the well-stocked, decorative potager. Completing the picture is a circular rose garden filled with fragrant David Austin roses in pink and mauve, surrounded by nepeta, delphiniums and salvias – classics of an English garden.

RIGHT
Flowers, fruit, vegetables and herbs jostle in their box borders, creating patterns between the brick paths. The symmetry and subtle colours are a delight.

OPPOSITE, TOP
Espaliered apple trees surround the immaculate potager.

OPPOSITE, BOTTOM
Willow forms arches and plant supports in the potager, where chives, sweet peas and apple arches vie for attention.

15

Villa Ramsdal

CHELMSFORD, ESSEX

Villa Ramsdal, owned by Jerry and Marjorie Harpur since 1965, is a garden of memories. Jerry has always been interested in gardens, but lacks time. His wife, Marjorie, however, has gradually become a keen gardener, although she is very modest about her achievements. Christopher Masson designed a patio, semicircular path and beds by the back of the house, but the rest has evolved. Despite being a town garden, it has a relaxed style, with a vegetable plot and beds filled with cottage favourites and spring bulbs. Plants are chosen impulsively at garden centres, but roses and scent feature prominently. *Rosa* 'Wedding Day' creates a lovely shady arbour; 'Rambling Rector' climbs 12 metres (40 ft) into a pear tree. 'A friend gave me a cutting when it was a foot long', recalls Marjorie. People often give Jerry plants, too, as a reminder of various photographic jobs. The garden originated as a playing space for the Harpurs' four sons; now, on visits, they appreciate its restfulness. It is an extension to the house in summer and a place for the adventures of ten grandchildren to be remembered.

RIGHT
A restful seat at the back of the garden has a view of bright poppies and the scented *Rosa* 'Canary Bird'.

OPPOSITE, TOP LEFT
Rosa 'Rambling Rector' smothers a pear tree with small, creamy-white, semi-double flowers with a clove fragrance. It produces numerous small hips in autumn.

OPPOSITE, TOP RIGHT
Jerry and Marjorie's favourite rose, pink *Rosa* × *odorata* 'Mutabilis', is underplanted with herbs near their patio table. It flowers repeatedly from June until September.

OPPOSITE, BOTTOM
Pots are moved around to enhance the planting. Here, the different textures of leaves and petals – which have fascinated Jerry since he was a young child – are evident.

16

Chenies Manor

RICKMANSWORTH, BUCKINGHAMSHIRE

It is in large part because of the present
owner, Elizabeth MacLeod Matthews, that
the gardens surrounding Chenies Manor
are so spectacular. They are divided into
compartments connected by archways, and
united by the clever use of grass and low
box hedging. Shrubs and herbaceous plants
flank seasonal plantings. In May the tulips
of every colour and form that fill the sunken
garden are breathtaking, and surprisingly
harmonious. Frothy forget-me-nots act as a
foil, but at the end of the month they and
the tulips are replaced with tender perennials.
Beside a white garden, yew-topiary birds
perch on large yew plinths on the lawn.
Yew also creates a maze, based on a unique
triangular pattern. Near by is an iron gazebo
painted palest grey–green, rather than
harsher, more typical white. In the walled
kitchen garden, cordons of gooseberries and
currants stand by rhubarb forced in large
terracotta pots. The juxtaposition of restraint
and exuberance is maintained to the last.

The sunken garden is modelled on
a Tudor privy garden. In spring it is
filled with tulips, arrayed in blocks
of around twenty of each variety,
offsetting trim lawn and clipped box.

OPPOSITE
Simple wooden arches draped in ivy (seen here) and hooped arches covered in clematis beckon to different areas of the garden. A dark yew hedge on the left of the sunken garden allows the planting to shine.

FAR LEFT
Tulipa 'Queen of Sheba' is combined with forget-me-nots. The latter are grown each year from seed in greenhouses in the garden, to maintain the perfect blue.

LEFT
Tulipa 'Pink Impression'.

BELOW, LEFT
A colourful mixed border of tulips and forget-me-nots, fronted by an unusual combination of bergenia and orange pansies.

BELOW
The double, white, peony-flowered *Tulipa* 'Mount Tacoma' blooms in late April and May.

63

17

Lamorran House Gardens

ST MAWES, CORNWALL

This garden is arresting on many levels. Its location is particularly spectacular, on a south-facing slope, with water on three sides glimpsed at first, but gradually coming into view as you descend, giving the illusion of being on a Mediterranean peninsula. Planting is subtropical and luxuriant, with many tree ferns and the largest collection of palm trees in England. There is also a Japanese influence in the many azaleas and rhododendrons. More unexpected is the Italianate atmosphere achieved by the designer and owner, Robert Dudley-Cooke, who, with his Italian wife, has lived here for twenty-eight years, and whose aim was to create a family garden. Not only the myriad Mediterranean plants but also the hard landscaping of arches, balustrades, columns and statues enhance the garden and provide intimacy. Gravel paths and steps zigzag down the steep hillside between enclosed areas in a journey of discovery. The garden is 1.6 hectares (4 acres), but the impression is of a greater space. Streams and tranquil pools among the planting add another element of surprise to this unique garden.

RIGHT
A view across the bay is framed by tall pillars. Yuccas and palms are typical of the largely evergreen planting, with lawns kept to a minimum.

OPPOSITE
The garden's microclimate is increased with planting and climate change. When palms were first put in, they just about survived; now they romp away. Here they stand sentinel beside a flight of steps under an arch, with a view over the lower garden to St Anthony Head.

Koi carp circle contentedly in their
secluded but impressive pool.

OPPOSITE
'My parents were very keen
herbaceous gardeners, and I am
exactly the opposite', says Robert
Dudley-Cooke. His interests are
more architectural in both planting
and hard landscaping, illustrated
here by the ferns and bamboos as
well as the elaborate water feature.

18

Inner Temple

LONDON

A notice on the black wrought-iron railings that enclose this 'secret' oasis in central London reads: '12.30–3. Outside of these hours, only Residents and Masters of the Bench are permitted to enter the Garden.' And indeed there is a special atmosphere within this garden, which has existed since medieval times. It is surrounded by the Inns of Court, and peopled largely by men, and some dark-suited women. Judge Simon Brown QC, Master of the Garden, says: 'Over the centuries, the gardens have been the setting for declarations of love and war; revels, parties and shows; quiet contemplation, study, discussion and exercise.' Literary figures who mention the garden in their works include Shakespeare, Milton, Boswell, Thackeray and Dickens. Today the ample borders have a relaxed feel. Herbaceous plants and roses are supplemented with annuals for continuous seasonal interest. Forget-me-nots and tulips might be replaced by dahlias and zinnias, or painted sage and *Nicotiana mutabilis*. Plane trees dating from the 1870s and rare specimen trees enhance the large central lawn, sweeping towards the Thames.

RIGHT
A magnificent *Magnolia salicifolia* is clothed in masses of star-shaped, fragrant, pure-white flowers.

OPPOSITE
The High Border changes subtly with each season and is the 'pride and joy' of the head gardener, Andrea Brunsendorf. In late summer it is still a vibrant composition, with dark-blue *Salvia guaranitica* 'Blue Enigma', tall *Helianthus* 'Lemon Queen', golden *Rudbeckia fulgida* var. *deamii*, orange *Helenium* 'Sahin's Early Flowerer', dark *Dahlia* 'Nuit d'Eté' and, in the background, the exotic cones of *Echium pininana*.

19

Hatch End

NUN MONKTON, NORTH YORKSHIRE

Mr and Mrs Beaumont bought their seventeenth-century cottage on the village green in 1996 and got on with the garden straight away, already knowing much of what they wanted to achieve. Mrs Beaumont is a potter, so art and form come naturally to her. The atmospheric 0.25-hectare (⅝-acre) garden surrounds the house and has many distinct areas, including a croquet lawn, four large colour-themed beds, a potager and a herb garden. But it is topiary that creates the most dramatic feature of the garden, especially the parterre at the front of the house, in seven different shades of green. Mrs Beaumont loves the neatness and control of box and clipped hedging, as well as ebullient planting, and relishes her mystical garden, where she claims children can imagine dragons hiding in the beds. She says: 'It is a great privilege to be able to do what we have done. It is not every day that you can find a property with this potential.'

RIGHT
This striking box parterre at the front of the house was partly inspired by the work of Arabella Lennox-Boyd, but was designed and planted by Julie Beaumont. It was made from cuttings taken from existing box trees in the garden, which rooted readily.

OPPOSITE, TOP
A serpentine lawn and bronze-leaved *Prunus* 'Kanzan' act as foils to a tall beech hedge and topiary in pots.

OPPOSITE, BOTTOM
The front garden is on the village green, so everyone who passes has a chance to be wowed by the parterre.

BELOW, FROM TOP
Rosmarinus officinalis Prostrate Group;
Anthemis tinctoria 'E.C. Buxton'.

RIGHT
A problem with standing water was solved by planting a herb garden in raised square brick beds and large terracotta pots.

OPPOSITE, TOP
A snaking yew hedge leads to the side entrance of the house. It is an area of great calm.

OPPOSITE, BOTTOM
Structure and texture play important roles throughout. Here, too, predominantly yellow flowers are complemented by shades of green, grey and white.

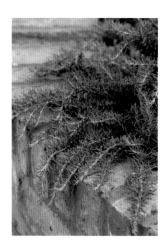

20

Rolls Farm

HAVERHILL, ESSEX

Trees, colour, shape and space all play a part
in the success of this elegant family country
garden, designed by Nicky Baker. In summer,
rectangular box-bordered beds in front of the
house hold a delicious combination of rich
plum dahlias, thalictrum and echinacea, in
front of rows of silver birch by black sheds.
Beside the house, a rose tunnel leads to a
small knot garden of variegated greens in-
filled with gravel, the sides softened with
mauve catmint, verbena, irises and wisteria.
Behind the rose-clad house, a circular lawn is
encircled with more roses and perennials, and
box balls line steps leading to a larger lawn,
edged with trees and shrubs, with open fields
and a wild-flower meadow beyond, ending
with a weeping willow. Mowing is carefully
controlled, with areas of long grass creating
patterns and contrast. In winter it is structure
that comes to the fore: rows of bare trees and
clipped evergreens – the bones of the garden
– are shown to their full advantage. Although
each side of the house has a different garden,
there are no rooms or water features. This is
both a personal and a classic English garden,
with carefully chosen ironwork throughout,
black-painted outbuildings, and – in the
warmer months – a wealth of butterflies.

An avenue of fastigiate prunus
trees to the side of the garden is
mesmerizingly beautiful in winter.
Softer beeches edge the simple
skeletal structure of the trees, which
grow fainter as they disappear into a
background of sky and frosted grass.

A semicircular white wrought-iron seat stands out against a silhouetted apple tree. The grass is allowed to grow longer here, catching frost in the shelter of a hedge of wild plum.

The circular garden forces boundaries outwards. Raised beds in a semicircle are planted for seasonal structure. Box balls lead to the spreading oak tree, while a library, table-tennis room and tool shed on the left recede.

This is a garden for play, too: here a Wendy house; and by the circular garden is a sandpit.

21

Bourton House

BOURTON-ON-THE-HILL,
GLOUCESTERSHIRE

Perhaps above all, Bourton House garden, although large and varied, achieves a sense of harmony. Ironwork throughout is by Richard Overs, and shapes are repeated so that flamboyancy is anchored by structure. Squares and rectangles are used in the knot garden, large lawn, raised walk, potager and white garden, in sympathy with the lines of the early eighteenth-century house. Conversely, uprights, such as arches, arbours, fences and yew hedges, all echo a wavy ogival (onion) shape, adding a softer resonance. Monique and Richard Paice have owned Bourton House for twenty-six years, and it is largely Monique who has designed and developed the garden. Borders are mainly colour-schemed, and different areas are approached as a surprise, through dark yew hedging. It was also Monique's idea to move a huge bath-like stone basket, used as a raised pond, to the centre of the knot garden. Now the exuberance of its fountainous planting contrasts wonderfully with the surrounding formality, transforming calming green to an area of excitement – typical of this unusual garden.

RIGHT
Terraces were created to give more opportunity for planting, especially low-growing shrubs. *Chamerion dodonaei* sprawls at the front, with *Monarda* 'Croftway Pink' and the spikes of white *Veronicastrum virginicum* 'Album' and blue *Veronica exaltata*; at the back is *Fuchsia magellanica*.

OPPOSITE, TOP
The house, first Tudor, then fortified Jacobean, now dates principally from around 1710. The south façade looks out on to lawn and mixed borders, here showing an attractive late-summer combination of mauve perovskia, pink buddleia and yellow rudbeckia.

OPPOSITE, BOTTOM
Shallow stone steps lead to the eighteenth-century raised walk overlooking rolling hills, framed by ironwork by Richard Overs.

OPPOSITE, TOP
The knot garden, planted with low
box hedging with variegated box
pyramids, has bark-covered earth
inside, rather than flowers. Ivy has
been trained to cover an arbour of
arresting design, adding more shapes
and textures of green.

OPPOSITE, BOTTOM, AND LEFT
A multitude of terracotta pots
provides homes for more tender
plants. Geraniums, fuchsias and
succulents are skilfully placed, and
a delightful pair of box hens with
chicks peck in a planter.

ABOVE
Beside the white garden is a cool
green corridor consisting of a gravel
path bordered by box and terracotta
pots filled with daisies.

22

Glebe Place, Chelsea
LONDON

The inspiration for this garden came from
a burglar. Martin Summers and his wife live
in a unique house converted from artists'
studios. Their bedroom has French windows
to the roof, and one night, a burglar entered.
When Martin tackled him, the thief pleaded
for leniency, promising to share a tip for
preventing future intrusion. He suggested
2.5-metre (8-ft) trellising around the roof,
and a stunning haven was born. Uneven
levels enable different parts of the roof
garden, even within an area just 3 by
36.5 metres (10 by 120 ft). Half-concealed
mirrors add light and the illusion of space.
Some 3000 pots containing trees, climbers,
shrubs, annuals and perennials – all hand-
watered – stand on artificial grass. Four
replica minarets from Brighton Pavilion
(used there while the originals were repaired)
sit astride the gables, and informed the
oriental flavour throughout, with fifty small
statues of Buddha, wind chimes and pools.
Calm and seclusion, not ostentation, abide,
although Rod Stewart, Mick Jagger, Lucian
Freud and Jack Nicholson have all sat here.
The garden has given much joy, but Martin
remarks ruefully, 'When we leave, I can't
expect other people to maintain my dream.'

RIGHT
Plants of almost every type and
colour (although purple is a
favourite and orange disliked) thrive
in terracotta pots placed on the
floor or hung from the trellis of this
sun-trapped roof terrace. Roses,
fuchsia, clematis, robinia, hydrangea,
hebe, petunia and hardenbergia are
just a few.

OPPOSITE
Steps lead to seating areas. On the
left is the glass ceiling of the triple-
height studio, now a tented living
room. One of the minarets houses
a concealed speaker, which plays
the dawn chorus during the day
and cicadas at night. Concealed
lighting adds to the enchantment.

23

Sissinghurst Castle Garden

CRANBROOK, KENT

Perhaps the most famous, most copied, most visited and best-loved garden in England is that created by writer Vita Sackville-West and her husband, Harold Nicolson: Sissinghurst. Its romantic setting and atmosphere, its combination of profuse, soft planting with a formal framework, and its intimate 'garden rooms' form a peerless whole and a unique experience for the visitor. Vita and Harold moved to Sissinghurst in 1932 and developed the 3.6-hectare (9-acre) garden around the surviving parts of an Elizabethan mansion. Walls and clipped yew hedges are used extensively to create enclosed spaces linked by surprise vistas formed by arches and gaps in the boundaries. Not only do roses scramble up the brick walls, but there is also a lovely old-fashioned rose garden, together with a vibrant cottage garden, the poetic and influential white garden, a lime walk, a fragrant herb garden, an orchard, a wild-flower meadow and a moat. Collectively, they create what has been described as 'a triumphant essay in English style'.

The walled garden seen from the Tudor tower. Yew hedging provides vital structure, in what Vita Sackville-West described as 'the strictest formality of design, with the maximum informality of planting'. To the left is the yellow, orange and red cottage garden, and to the right, the rondel and rose garden.

OPPOSITE, TOP
The wonderful white garden with *Rosa mulliganii* in full bloom on the pergola. In the foreground are *Lilium regale* among silver-leaved *Lychnis coronaria* 'Alba'. To the left is South Cottage, where Vita and Harold had their bedrooms.

OPPOSITE, BOTTOM
Phygelius, clematis and asters in hot colours contrast with the cool of the white garden, glimpsed through the brick archway.

ABOVE
The cottage garden – which is not traditional at all in its inclusion of tender exotics and its sunset colour scheme – is seen across Sissinghurst Crescent (so nicknamed by Harold, who designed it).

RIGHT
North-west from the white garden is an old arched gate in a clematis-clad brick wall.

24

Blakenham Woodland Garden

IPSWICH, SUFFOLK

There is something magical about good woodland gardens, where, in an atmosphere both natural and heightened, one can almost imagine seeing an elf or a fairy. Blakenham – a wonderful combination of traditional English woodland and many exotic trees and shrubs, planted over fifty years – is one such garden. The wooded hill was bought by the late John Blakenham, treasurer of the Royal Horticultural Society and owner of the adjacent house. Clearing brambles and nettles, he created glades of bluebells; and, finding the soil acid, he was also able to plant rare magnolias, azaleas and camellias given to him by like-minded plantsmen friends. His son Michael has increased the stock of trees and shrubs, while Michael's wife, an artist and potter, has contributed to the aesthetics and atmosphere of the garden, so that wild campion and foxgloves seem effortlessly to harmonize with bamboo, sculptures and Chinese rocks. In the middle of the garden is a delightful surprise: a stunning grass landform spiralling down as if into a plughole.

RIGHT
Naturalized bluebells as far as the eye can see remain one of the great delights of the woodland garden.

OPPOSITE, TOP LEFT
A mown path cut through a meadow of buttercups, daisies and cow parsley near the house adds another dimension of the natural and tamed.

OPPOSITE, TOP RIGHT
By the house is a smaller area of more traditional garden. Designer Rosemary Verey advised on the creation of the potager, which is perfect in style and structure, combining utility and beauty.

OPPOSITE, BOTTOM
A glorious combination of bluebells and the emerging pink-tinged foliage of *Aesculus parviflora* creates the impression of a pool within a sea.

OPPOSITE, TOP
At the heart of the wood is a tilting landform ringed with sycamores. Inspired by the landforms of Charles Jencks, it spirals down to a chalk 'plughole', adding an element of surprise, fun and beauty.

OPPOSITE, BOTTOM
Around a tree, a grass seat is formed from woven willow and grass. Hazel uprights form the 'chair' back, creating an unusual setting from which to contemplate the mysterious wood.

ABOVE
An imaginatively clipped yew hedge separates the lawn and formal gardens from the wood, the entrance to which – almost like a door to Narnia – is beyond.

RIGHT
A sculptural piece of natural stone is supported on a willow-covered plinth.

25

The Jungle Garden
NORWICH, NORFOLK

The idea for this garden evolved after trips to Thailand and Bali, as well as to Will Giles's garden near by (70). Jon Kelf created his garden, measuring just 18 by 8 metres (60 by 26 ft), behind his modern house in the suburbs of Norwich. Moving in twelve years ago, he was confronted by a slope of bare earth, and decided to dig out five terraced levels. At first he laid lawn, adding bedding plants and conifers. Dissatisfied, he replaced the grass with decking, and the bedding with more than 200 exotics, including palms, bamboos, ferns and bananas: a feast of form and texture. Such a garden requires little maintenance, mainly trimming off dead leaves in spring. Nothing gets winter protection, since the mass planting provides a microclimate: even bananas subjected to frost are cut back to the ground and shoot up again. But it is the inspired combination of exotic plants with airy decked terraces in a small garden that creates a piece of paradise.

RIGHT, TOP
On the fifth terrace is a hut-like gazebo surrounded by dicksonias (tree ferns). Almost the whole garden can be seen from here.

RIGHT
Hedychium densiflorum (hardy ginger) creates a striking flame of orange against the green foliage.

FAR RIGHT
The front of the house, with its enticing screen of cordyline, *Canna indica*, juniper, phormium and palm, invites exploration of what lies at the back.

OPPOSITE, TOP
The tropical feeling is heightened and unity provided by bamboo rails. The sunny main deck is partially shaded at midday by a large robinia.

OPPOSITE, BOTTOM
Weathered decking provides a wonderful backdrop for the fronds of jungle foliage.

In the evening, with LED lighting and spotlights throughout, the garden and its varied seating areas take on a new magic.

26

Manor House

WILTSHIRE

This is an extravagant garden in every sense of the word. When Isabel and Julian Bannerman were asked to redevelop a farmhouse and its 2-hectare (5-acre) garden, their boldness was unstinting. They delight in dramatic effect, and were inspired by Forde Abbey, where an older building was 'Georgianized' (97); here, the reverse is true, so it appears that a monastic garden pre-dates the house. Following eighteenth-century tradition, towers, arches and ruined follies have been created from salvaged and new stone, with lime mortar. As well as a cloister garden, there is a surprise Italianate roof garden, with fountain pools surrounded by box and blue and white annual and herbaceous plants. Skilful use is made throughout of box hedges, yew cones, rambling and shrub roses (white and pink), self-seeded plants (especially successful in the walls) and scented flowers. The other side of the house provides a contrasting atmosphere: an elegant pool, with arched recesses, obelisks, a thatched boathouse and wisteria pergolas, is inspired by the gardens of Portugal. All aspects amaze in this true fantasy garden.

RIGHT, TOP
The formality of the parterre makes a fitting entrance to the cloister; the effect is softened with roses.

RIGHT, BOTTOM
The three pools of the Italianate roof garden are surrounded by clipped box and contrasting clouds of nigella and daisies.

OPPOSITE, TOP
Self-seeded valerian and Mexican daisies combine with roses to smother the 'ruin', making it look as though it has been there for ever.

OPPOSITE, BOTTOM LEFT
Startlingly colourful tulips enliven the green of the topiary in the parterre.

OPPOSITE, BOTTOM RIGHT
Stone arches are echoed with clipped cones of yew.

OPPOSITE, TOP
Balustrading runs along a loggia terrace with steps each side leading to a formal pool.

OPPOSITE, BOTTOM
The pool impresses, with two obelisks supporting spouting bull's heads, and a thatched boathouse of sandblasted green oak.

LEFT
The loggia terrace is crowded with herbs, such as rosemary and lavender, and the roses 'Buff Beauty' (foreground) and 'Crépuscule', which fill the air with scent.

27

Helmingham Hall

STOWMARKET, SUFFOLK

For wow-factor alone, Helmingham Hall
excels: this is dreaming on a grand and lavish
scale. The gardens were redesigned by Lady
Xa Tollemache (garden designer and wife
of the owner) to complement the Hall
of 1510, with its patterned brick, moat
and drawbridge. Two areas are particularly
impressive: the knot garden and the walled
garden. The first, framed by dark yew
hedging, is made up of four box squares
between grass paths. Each contains a unique,
intricate pattern of intertwining box, with
delicate planting in the sections between.
Behind are two rectangular beds of roses,
also bordered by box. Contrasting long
grass, strewn with wild flowers, edges the
inner moat, with bridges leading to gates
into the *pièce de résistance*: the walled garden.
Immaculate cruciform beds hold flowers,
fruit and vegetables in opulent profusion.
In the borders, grasses and herbaceous
perennials of all colours cavort in soft
mounds, spires and spikes. Outside the
walls are more borders, where repetition
brings cohesion to the bravura planting.

RIGHT
A mown path meanders through a
wild-flower meadow and orchard at
the edge of the deer park, providing
an area of contrast with the more
formal parts of the garden.

OPPOSITE, TOP
The walled garden here is thought
to be of Saxon origin, to protect
stock from marauders. Now it
holds a medley of fruit and flowers,
including exceptional mixed borders,
within its magnificent gates.

OPPOSITE, BOTTOM
Borders increase in vibrancy as
summer progresses, with dot-
plantings of annuals extending the
season. Here, delphiniums, achillea,
poppies, alstroemeria and *Salvia sclarea*
var. *turkestanica* provide the spectacle.

OPPOSITE, TOP
On the west side of the house is a classic parterre, redesigned in 1987. Box hedging is filled with soft, grey *Santolina chamaecyparissus*, with white cosmos forming a circle in the centre.

OPPOSITE, BOTTOM
A wide grass causeway, flanked by striking egg-shaped domes of yew and bordered by rougher grass scattered with ox-eye daisies (*Leucanthemum vulgare*), separates the inner and outer moats.

RIGHT
In the walled garden, rusted iron arches form tunnels over calming turf paths leading to eight separate sections. At different times of year the tunnels are festooned with roses, vines, sweet peas, runner beans or (as here) — unusually, and to great effect — with gourds. The seat was designed by George Carter.

28

Chapel Street

HACONBY, LINCOLNSHIRE

The Curtises had no particular aim when they made their garden on this 0.2-hectare (½-acre) plot, formerly a smallholding. Like many gardeners, they buy plants and then create places for them. But that has resulted in a varied, attractive garden. It runs along a north–south axis but is also on a slope in the same direction, so is better drained at the bottom. The front is dry and sunny, and the drive has been cleverly extended to create gravel beds. Here, too, every imaginable container is used to grow alpines. Gravel paths continue through perennials, in a cottage-style garden, where asters are a favourite. Finally there is a woodland area planted, in particular, with snowdrops. Mr and Mrs Curtis love the variety of plants one can grow now. They considered living abroad, but would miss England's seasons, and sitting enjoying a cup of tea in their garden, surrounded by their labour of love.

RIGHT, TOP
A passion for plants is matched only by a passion for old signs and containers. A fabulous backdrop has been created for pots, millstones and cattle troughs displaying alpines.

RIGHT, BOTTOM
Drifts of late-summer perennials in the gravel garden include miscanthus, salvia and sedum.

OPPOSITE, TOP
In true cottage style, everything is packed in here. Asteraceae are particularly loved, with cosmos, *Aster* 'Little Carlow' and many dahlias – among them 'Lilac Time', 'Bishop of Llandaff', 'Tally Ho', 'Dark Desire' and 'David Howard'. *Robinia pseudoacacia* 'Frisia' and *Sambucus nigra* f. *porphyrophylla* 'Black Lace' overhang.

OPPOSITE, BOTTOM LEFT, FROM TOP
Salvia leucantha; a dahlia seedling fortuitously found in the garden.

OPPOSITE, BOTTOM RIGHT
A table under the apple tree makes picking dessert a pleasure, while surrounding plants, including Japanese anemones and the umbrellas of *Darmera peltata*, add seclusion.

29

Little Ponton Hall

GRANTHAM, LINCOLNSHIRE

Although Little Ponton Hall has many attractions – a 200-year old cedar, a river walk, a walled garden, a listed stone dovecote and a Victorian greenhouse – it is loveliest in winter, when snowdrops and aconites create a closely woven, shimmering carpet of white and gold over ancient woodland earth and spacious lawns. There are several gardens renowned for snowdrops, but winter aconites receive less reverence, despite their heart-warming cheer. Both flowers have been here for as long as anyone can remember, and Mrs McCorquodale has lived at Little Ponton Hall for eighty-five years, and her parents before her. She became interested in gardening in middle age, but is now very keen. She has made particular improvements to the walled garden, creating different sections, adding yew hedges and introducing many old, perfumed French roses, clematis, peonies and a herb garden. Admitting that 'gardening never ends', she has just ordered some *Rosa rugosa*, continuing the combination of wild and cultivated, formal and relaxed, that gives this garden its enduring charm and sense of contentment.

The house was originally built in 1640, and has Georgian and later additions. It sits in the bottom of a valley, where a stream runs into the River Witham. Under a chestnut tree, snowdrops (*Galanthus nivalis*) and aconites (*Eranthis hyemalis*) mingle in glorious, uninhibited profusion.

30

The Magic Garden
WOLVERHAMPTON, WEST MIDLANDS

The Magic Garden is aptly named, holding unexpected delights. At 23 by 6 metres (75 by 20 ft), it is a typical Victorian town garden, except that it is walled. Bob Parker and Greg Kowalczuk have divided it into five parts, with curving diagonal boundaries, giving the garden a much wider appearance. A patio by the house leads to a terracotta area, edged with tiles from the old kitchen and adorned with finials from Victorian houses. Next is a pool garden, and beyond, a wild woodland area of trees and bamboos. The whole garden is shady, except the formal 'rosary' at the end, and throughout are *objets trouvés*, such as railway and police lanterns, wheels, chimney pots and masks. With so much to look at, there is a restraining emphasis on green plants. Bob delights in texture, design and surprises, more than flowers. There is a one-way system for visitors, who must exit at the back, but many walk round the cul-de-sac and come in again, lots of them several times – and no wonder.

RIGHT
Twice a year, at night, lanterns, candles, torches and low-voltage bulbs illuminate the truly magical garden. There are over 1000 lights, taking more than two and half hours to light. People queue to visit, saying it reminds them of waiting to see Santa's grotto as children.

OPPOSITE, TOP
The terracotta garden is bordered by hostas, ferns and Solomon's seal. Tall plants are not always kept to the back of the densely planted beds. An iron gate leads to the water garden.

OPPOSITE, BOTTOM
In the rosary garden, clematis grows on chains strung between posts. A central ivy-clad pillar holds an armillary sphere, while above the Lutyens-style seat hangs a Victorian carriage wheel like a spider's web amongst the ivy, conifers and ferns.

31

Hestercombe

CHEDDON FITZPAINE, SOMERSET

Hestercombe is a unique combination of three gardens spanning three centuries of English garden history and design. The Georgian Landscape Garden, like a landscape painting, offers eye-catching composed views complete with a lake, a cascade, woodland, temples and grottoes. On the south side of the house is the Victorian Terrace Garden, an array of colourful bedding. Last, but perhaps best, is the Edwardian Formal Garden, created by the famous working partnership of architect Edwin Lutyens and painter-turned-plantswoman Gertrude Jekyll. Lutyens, a master in the use of local materials, employed stone and tiles for his signature semicircular steps, a pool and rills, and a long, handsome pergola that frames the Taunton Vale. Drifts of Jekyll's sensuous planting soften the effect, and everywhere in paths, walls and steps are the pretty daisy flowers of *Erigeron karvinskianus*.

The nineteenth-century house was designed by E.W. Portman. The Formal Garden, laid out between 1904 and 1908, and including this sunken area with fountain and rill, is considered by many to be the finest example of the partnership between Lutyens and Jekyll.

Attention to detail and variety in hard landscaping were crucial to Lutyens. The pergola, which forms a boundary to the garden, is composed alternately of round and square pillars of horizontally stacked slate. Roses, clematis and lavender enhance the design.

Masses of evergreen bergenia are typical of Jekyll, who favoured borders of hardy flowers. The art of planting with scintillating combinations of colour and texture is her enduring legacy.

The 16-hectare (40-acre) Landscape Garden in the Combe Valley, north of the house, was designed between 1759 and 1786 by the then owner, Coplestone Warre Bampfylde, to give an impression of an idealized classical landscape with a lake, a temple, trees and shrubs, but few flowers.

32

Middleton Hall

SUDBURY, SUFFOLK

Mr and Mrs Allen moved to Middleton Hall in 1994, after twenty years spent in rented accommodation abroad. The garden was then 3 hectares (7½ acres), but they have added a hectare and reworked most of the design. Because the back of the house dates from the 1540s, they wanted a Tudor-style garden there, and employed Mark Rumary of Notcutts to design one, re-creating Tudor layout and using herbaceous and annual plants that would have grown in that period (advised by Rosemary Verey). This is still the outstanding feature of the garden, but it is joined by an impressive potager, a shady wood and a cascading water feature, for past and present sit together happily here. The Allens admit that they are not obsessive gardeners, but they particularly enjoy the peaceful silence of the Tudor garden, where the borders make a tapestry contained within a formal structure.

RIGHT, TOP
The impressive back of the house, made of timber and patterned brick, dates from Tudor times. In the Tudor garden, box, herbs, Rosa Mundi (*Rosa gallica* 'Versicolor') and lavender provide a heady fragrance in summer.

RIGHT, BOTTOM
Raised wooden beds of fruit and vegetables grown in succession stand on gravel paths in the potager, with obelisks of sweet peas.

OPPOSITE
The Tudor garden, seen from the house. At its centre is an antique carved-stone wellhead, and in each corner stands a bespoke painted wooden heraldic beast on a green-and-white pole (far left). Behind is a 'flowery mead', where 11,000 daffodils march down the hill in spring.

33

Tilford Cottage

FARNHAM, SURREY

There is a surprise around every corner at Tilford. The owner, artist Rod Burn, who dreamed up the garden over the past fifteen years, wanted to transform empty fields into a garden that could hold 300 people without their being seen. As a result, living-willow screens and hedges of beech, yew, thuja, box and cotoneaster create partitions between areas. These include a vibrant herbaceous garden, a symbolic holistic garden, a perfect hosta garden and a beautiful herb garden. In a wild area beside the River Wey, aspen, willow and Joe Pye weed (*Eupatorium*) rustle in the breeze, and cinnabar-moth caterpillars merge with yellow ragwort. All the senses are stimulated, with wind chimes heard faintly throughout. Sculpture and topiary play prominent and amusing parts, too. Golden yew birds strut by the house. A square of clipped box in front of a bench can support a tea tray. Stones are placed in trees, pebbles hang from strings, and topiarized figures emerge from hedges. The aim of this garden is tranquillity as well as quirkiness, wonder and inspiration: it succeeds.

RIGHT, TOP
The thyme walk is edged with a tree trunk supporting a stone and chiselled cedar sculptures by Rod Burn. Hues of grey and pink are heightened by the addition of purple–bronze *Cotinus* 'Grace'.

RIGHT, BOTTOM
A boardwalk with chestnut railing runs along the River Wey at the bottom of the garden. It is in the Japanese style, following the belief that if a path is not straight, spirits will not follow you.

OPPOSITE
Paths, too, are unusual in this garden. Below variegated maples, and beside a curving thuja hedge, is a path made of 'cobbles' of black cherry wood.

OPPOSITE, TOP
A grass path leads from a lawn near the house to the wild garden. It is bordered with striking *Salix integra* 'Hakuro-nishiki' in front of a tunnel of wisteria.

OPPOSITE, BOTTOM
In a wilder area, a wooden bridge spans the bog garden, with mixed grasses in front and woodland behind.

BELOW
A yew gatekeeper guards one of the three blue doors leading to the secret herb garden.

RIGHT
Through a door in the herb garden, arched with *Humulus lupulus* 'Aureus', is a knot garden. A seated figure (a likeness of Rod himself) of shrubby honeysuckle (*Lonicera nitida*) surveys the scene. It has taken seven years for him to reach this life-like maturity.

34

Easton Lodge

GREAT DUNMOW, ESSEX

Everything at Easton Lodge is on a vast scale, so the impression is that one has stepped into a garden for giants in a bygone age. The most important parts of this 14-hectare (35-acre) garden are those designed by Harold Peto in 1902. There remain a formal croquet lawn (more suited in scale, perhaps, for football); an elegant sunken Italian garden, containing a 30.5-metre-long (100 ft) balustraded lily pool; and a pretty courtyard of herringbone brick and cobbles behind Warwick House (which replaces the original lodge). It was this courtyard that Brian and Diana Creasey fell in love with when they arrived in 1971 and began restoring the garden. With pavilions, terraced beds, a glade, a bosquet, a large fishing lake, a walk of towering pines, a lime tunnel and, appropriately, a mass of giant hogweed, it is a grand undertaking. Varying owners, war, storms and diminishing funds have taken their toll on the garden, but Brian Creasey's passion has not faltered. His dream is that the whole will emerge from the romantic ruin I visited, to become the glorious garden that is waiting to bloom.

There has been a deer park at Easton Lodge since 1302, but its heyday was the early 1900s, when Daisy, Countess of Warwick (at one time mistress of Edward, Prince of Wales) commissioned Harold Peto to construct extensive gardens. Men from the Salvation Army Inebriates' Home carried out the construction work. Much of Peto's scheme has now been uncovered, including the Italian garden, shown here, which, despite requiring restoration, retains a faded splendour.

35

The Beth Chatto Gardens

ELMSTEAD MARKET, ESSEX

Beth Chatto, doyenne gardener and writer, is famous for her use of the right plant in the right place. Her garden began in 1960, from a wasteland, and combines conditions of dry and damp soil in both sun and shade; but she has miraculously created an immaculate garden overflowing with plants. The gravel garden was once a car park. Neither fed nor watered, it is home to mounds of drought-tolerant perennials, annuals, grasses and succulents of all colours. Movement, vertical accents and texture are all incorporated, with such plants as *Stipa gigantea* and lavender punctuated by prickly eryngium and the woolly spires of verbascum. Gravel paths give way to mown grass on the descent to the water garden, where lush marginal plants border four interconnecting ponds. A quieter atmosphere prevails, although unity is achieved through the continued island beds and the emphasis on shape and texture. Completing this show garden, a treasure trove of ideas to be 'borrowed', is a shady woodland area, which, although planted, feels much wilder.

RIGHT
In the gravel garden a fastigiate yew forms the tallest and darkest accent, allowing *Yucca gloriosa* 'Variegata' to shine, while thrift (*Armeria maritima*) adds a splash of pink below.

OPPOSITE, TOP
The garden is not simply an experiment in the survival of the fittest, but also a crafting of associations of form, with plants that look good all year even with little maintenance. A favourite plant for impact is yellow kniphofia.

OPPOSITE, BOTTOM
The inspiration for this garden was a dry riverbed in New Zealand, where plants flowed over the inhospitable banks. Here, a tapestry of planting includes lime-green *Euphorbia characias* subsp. *wulfenii*, *Allium hollandicum* 'Purple Sensation', *Phlomis russeliana* and orange *Papaver atlanticum* 'Flore Pleno', with bearded irises.

In the water garden, here shaded by oaks, the stream flows past pink candelabra primulas and yellow irises, and the contrasting large-leaved skunk cabbage, *Lysichiton americanus*.

OPPOSITE, BOTTOM, FROM LEFT
Yellow and orange crown imperials (*Fritillaria imperialis*) thrive beneath pink-flowered *Camellia* × *williamsii* 'Donation' in the woodland garden; bearded irises are happy in the dry garden, providing vibrant colour combined with the similar-leaved *Gladiolus communis* subsp. *byzantinus*; two sedums of different hues are separated by the billowing foliage of silvery *Artemisia* 'Powis Castle', grown in gravel.

LEFT
Various verticals, such as eryngium and agapanthus, lift the eye above carpets and mounds of plants beside and beneath. Beth Chatto thinks of plants as furniture in a room, creating focal points and different planes of vision.

127

36

The Lucy Redman School of Garden Design

RUSHBROOKE, SUFFOLK

Lucy Redman lives in a picture-postcard cottage, from which she runs her school, but she has more than an ordinary cottage garden: a small garden packed with big ideas. It is filled with plants, but also with sculpture, a chicken house, a round vegetable garden, a willow igloo and fun. In front of the house is a striking long border of red, white, green and purple shrubs, perennials and grasses. But, as Lucy points out, 'It is about texture and form, and if there are flowers too, that's a bonus.' Behind the house is more of a family garden, although it still contains huge variety, and the fact that Lucy is a plantswoman, a 'plantaholic' and a self-confessed 'maximalist' is evident. Plant combinations are superb, often including Lucy's favourite deep maroon (which matches her hair). She explains: 'I want the garden to be productive but pretty, original and inspiring. Sometimes I hardly sleep at night thinking up the next idea. It's a mad dream garden!' In fact, it is a garden where fantasy has been converted to enchanting reality.

RIGHT
Lucy made this stone parterre ('a traditional idea with a quirky twist'), of pebbles sunk into grass, in a pattern matching a 1930s gate. The cottage is of that period, and in order to link house and garden, she laid out the pattern in line with windows and walls. 'It looks lovely in winter when frost covers the grass but not the pebbles', she comments.

OPPOSITE, TOP
Rusted metal is much used, and to great effect. Here, a steel pergola clad with wisteria and passion flower frames the more formal back garden.

OPPOSITE, BOTTOM
The Walking Man by Maryanne Nicholls moves through a bed dominated by pinks, purples and white – the same colours that are in the kitchen, which looks out on to it. The scheme is achieved with *Stachys byzantina*, *Geranium palmatum* and campanula.

ABOVE
Arches of living willow form a
tunnel of green with a large willow
basket at the end, simply growing
into the ground: 'I don't like plinths.'

RIGHT
Naturalistic planting under
young trees.

FAR RIGHT
Cow parsley beneath a cherry tree is
divided by a wicker tunnel. Natural
materials are valued in this garden, as
is recycled metal: an old mower and
a plough breast – now sculptures –
were found on skips.

OPPOSITE, TOP
A grass seat surrounds an apple
tree, the original hazel now cleverly
replaced by woven rusty metal. It
provides a focal point, a resting place
(Beth Chatto has sat here) and a
children's climbing frame at the
end of the front garden.

OPPOSITE, BOTTOM
A willow arch leads to a personal
part of the garden. A mosaic path,
made from pebbles by Lucy and her
husband, is bordered by grey grass
under a copper beech. The grass
comes from the Falklands, where
Lucy's uncle fought in the war.

37

Broughton Castle

BANBURY, OXFORDSHIRE

When Lord Saye and Sele asked me, 'Does this qualify as a dream garden?' the answer was a resounding 'Yes'. The garden is elegant, tranquil, simple in structure and perfect in planting. It consists primarily of a walled garden (known as the Ladies' Garden), established in the 1880s, on the south side of the fourteenth-century castle, and herbaceous borders against the walls. Described thus the garden sounds very formal, and indeed there are straight lines and fleur-de-lys beds edged in clipped box, but all is softened by flowers spilling over gravel paths, and tantalizing views of the sublime enclosure through windows and arches in the wall. Reds and oranges are banned, and old-fashioned English flowers, particularly roses, have pride of place in the scheme. A remarkable combination of seclusion and openness exists, for uninterrupted views of the Oxfordshire countryside form a backdrop to this garden of dreamy colours, shapes and scents.

RIGHT
A view of the walled Ladies' Garden from the roof is like a painting. The formal box fleur-de-lys and circles contrast with the sprawling borders of roses, digitalis, nepeta, oenothera and sisyrinchium, contained by old walls and framed by the moat and serene countryside.

OPPOSITE, TOP
Wide, low, smoothly clipped box has a tactile quality, and the round beds planted with lavender are almost like pools of water.

OPPOSITE, BOTTOM
On the outer side of the Ladies' Garden, occasional windows allow glimpses of the delights within. Here, a stone bench is deliciously surrounded by white *Crambe cordifolia*, roses ('Albertine' on the wall and 'Marguerite Hilling' to the right), delphiniums, clematis, digitalis, astrantia and geraniums, in a colourwash of pink, mauve and blue.

BELOW, FROM TOP
Rosa gallica 'Versicolor' (Rosa Mundi);
R. 'Albertine'.

RIGHT
Beside the moat a grass path leads
under an arch smothered with old
roses. The planting is based on
advice given by Lanning Roper in
1970, but is now maintained by just
one gardener, with input from Lord
and Lady Saye and Sele.

OPPOSITE
Many people would be glad to
have a small part of this garden
as their whole. Artistry of plant
association is demonstrated
throughout, here combining alliums,
roses, salvia and penstemon with the
seed heads of aquilegia.

38

Marks Hall

COGGESHALL, ESSEX

This is an arboretum with a difference.
Within its 81 hectares (200 acres), trees
are planted geographically, and there is an
exciting, cutting-edge contemporary garden.
Year round, two large lakes reflect seasonal
planting. To the right of the upper lake is the
Millennium Walk, planted for autumn and
winter colour and scent: bright-stemmed
dogwood, white-trunked birch and heady
sarcococca punctuate swathes of mauve–buff
Miscanthus sinensis. Opposite, the walled garden,
open to the lake on one side, is fabulous in
spring and summer. A magnificent double
border incorporates fennel, santolina and
grasses, sparkling in silver and gold. In the
central garden of spheres, beneath amelanchier
trees, five stone and three box balls suggest a
giant game of bowls in progress. Alternating
stone and box blocks add striking symmetry,
against beds of purple, white and gold –
irises, verbena, lupins, anaphalis and monarda.
A meandering wall, looping through the area
like a snake, ends in a slate pool.

RIGHT, TOP
In the double border in the
eighteenth-century walled garden,
redesigned by Brita von Schoenaich,
hoar frost crystallizes the round seed
heads of *Phlomis samia* and the leaves
of rosemary and teucrium.

RIGHT, BOTTOM
Twin-stemmed cherry trees and
Rhododendron ponticum create strong
silhouettes in front of the spectral
lower lake and the walled garden.

OPPOSITE, TOP
As the sun rises on a frosty morning,
grasses (including *Stipa calamagrostis*)
are transformed into living, moving
sculptures, within a hornbeam hedge.

OPPOSITE, BOTTOM
An arched brick bridge and cascade
divide the two lakes. White-laced
European maples stand in undulating
frosted grass.

OVERLEAF
In winter, by the lower lake, a holly
tree, *Cortaderia selloana* (pampas
grass) and a weeping willow form
a feathery composition in sepia.

39

The Red House

BUNGAY, SUFFOLK

Tessa Hobbs (now a garden designer) and
her husband, Michael (ex-army), had lived
in seventeen houses with gardens before
moving to Suffolk. They felt the attractive
farmhouse, surrounded by fields of nettles,
looked uncomfortable and needed an
anchored setting. They made the garden
without much money, enjoying the process.
They determined on a bold parterre at
the front, first planted with pink roses and
red cotinus, but now – since Tessa decided
she could not bear the pink any longer –
sensationally filled with lavender. At the
back they kept horses and donkeys, and
at the side they made a terrace with roses,
and dug out an atmospheric, romantic
pond. This garden demonstrates the dictum
that if you don't succeed, try again, but
also celebrates the vision of its owners.
Gardeners are often instructed to plant for
all seasons; the roses and lavender used here
flower for a relatively short time, but in the
right season and with the right structure,
the result is breathtaking.

The side of the house is seen at
dusk, behind the unusually lovely
pond. A timber walkway painted in
Giverny-like green hugs the side of
the pond and ends in a balustraded
platform, providing a seating area
under the sycamore. Old-fashioned
roses are planted both by the pond
and next to the house.

The four octagonal beds of the south-west-facing parterre are edged with *Buxus sempervirens* and *B. sempervirens* 'Suffruticosa', providing a mix of greens. Grey is added to the palette with lavender foliage and santolina, planted around a central box pyramid. *Lavandula angustifolia* 'Hidcote' surrounds shorter, paler *L. angustifolia* 'Cedar Blue'. Tiny plants were used, and have meshed into this fabulous formal display: 'There was nothing casual about it', comments Tessa, who is also fastidious in cutting lavender back by the end of August. The front of the house is clad in mixed flowering climbers.

40

Goldens Barn

WETHERSFIELD, ESSEX

This spectacular and eclectic garden has evolved in size and scope during the past twenty years. Now 0.8 hectares (2 acres) – more than twice the original size – it includes a Mediterranean garden, herbaceous beds, two ponds, woodland and a stream. One of the earliest areas to be developed remains among the most beautiful, especially at its peak: a glorious wild-flower meadow, enhanced by standing stones and an obelisk. An outstanding feature of the garden is sculpture – sometimes inspired by holidays enjoyed by the owners, Mr and Mrs Springett. An existing beech-and-hazel hedge was shaped into waves by Mr Springett, who had a huge classical dragon's head and tail sculpted and fitted at either end. An old tree trunk has been carved by a chainsaw artist into an Easter Island head. On a mown bank, a 2-metre-long (6½ ft) reclining stone Buddha, bought in India, overlooks the garden.

RIGHT, TOP
Subsoil from digging a large pond was used to make banks and undulating land with low fertility, planted as a wonderful wild-flower meadow. An armillary-sphere sundial by David Harber, combining sculptural art with precision engineering, is strategically placed.

RIGHT, BOTTOM
An obelisk of mirrored glass, also by David Harber, creates both light and shadow. Every winter, the wild-flower meadow is cut down and raked, but in summer moonlight, Mike Springett describes the ox-eye daisies (*Leucanthemum vulgare*) as 'looking like snow on the ground'.

OPPOSITE
Bridges over the stream unite different areas of the garden. Beside this one is a magnificent Chinese dragon, half hedge and half sculpture. The wavy body, about 1.5 metres high and 45.5 metres long (5 ft by 150 ft), was cut by Mike. Failing to get a head for it from Beijing, he commissioned one locally, made from resin.

41

Ousden House

NEWMARKET, SUFFOLK

This large garden, which has evolved over the last fifteen years, demonstrates confidence and an adventurous spirit. One area flows into another with a sense of enjoyment rather than of control. Land has gradually been acquired so that the garden and park are now about 7.3 hectares (18 acres). Somewhat daunted at first, Mr and Mrs Robinson employed Arabella Lennox-Boyd to design the borders nearest the house. It was her idea to move the front door to the back and lift the sloping land to create a drive. The borders, rose garden, crinkle-crankle yew hedge, focal points and vistas combine to create a luxuriant effect, but it is the moat garden and lake that linger in the memory. A serpentine wooden walkway appears to float through the middle of the moat, surrounded by bog planting; at the end, stepping stones lead to a lookout seat. Descending, one enters a beech wood surrounding a magical lake, where silence reigns and reflected greens suffuse the evening light.

RIGHT
The brick house was once a stable block. *Rosa* 'New Dawn' on the wall, *R.* 'Felicia' beneath and shrub rose 'Buff Beauty' by the gatepost create a romantic entrance.

OPPOSITE, TOP
The rose garden contains mainly old-fashioned pink varieties with subtle herbaceous underplanting, against a background of clipped yew. Beds are edged with small bricks reclaimed from the old stable floor. *Rosa* 'Noisette Carnée' covers the central wooden arbour, with 'Irène Watts' at the foot of the pillars.

OPPOSITE, BOTTOM
The courtyard garden (now at the back of the house) was once a stable yard. The formality of low clipped box squares and balls and standard 'Iceberg' roses is softened by *Lavandula angustifolia* 'Hidcote' and nicotiana.

ABOVE
Once a commercial beech plantation, the area by the lake has been thinned of trees to banish straight lines. It is green in summer, and simply magnificent in autumn.

LEFT
It took a flood to make the owners realize that the bog garden would hold water: they then turned it into a fabulous moat. Planting is largely yellow, with irises, grasses, hosta and *Lysimachia punctata* on the left and self-seeded mimulus on the bridge. At the back, a lime tree is luminous in the sunlight.

OPPOSITE, TOP
The lake is overlooked by two horses, sculpted by Harriet Mead out of the scrap metal of Alfa Romeos. A car's radiator was used to make the mane.

OPPOSITE, BOTTOM
In spring, the banks of the lake are covered with bulbs. Here, in summer, a dinghy waits enticingly in glimmering green.

42

Gravetye Manor

EAST GRINSTEAD, WEST SUSSEX

Elizabethan Gravetye Manor was home to
William Robinson (1838–1935), renowned
gardener, writer and pioneer of the English
natural garden. It was here that many of his
ideas were fulfilled. Robinson was one of
the first practitioners of mixed herbaceous
borders, and it was he who helped vanquish
Victorian bedding schemes. Gravetye still
bears witness to Robinson's natural planting
schemes, with a refreshing lack of topiary,
statuary and fountains. Although some of the
beds have been replaced with lawn, there are
deep borders with dense drifts of perennials
among shrubs; a wild-flower meadow; an
area of trees, azaleas and rhododendrons;
and a lake. The wonderful high-walled
kitchen garden, its large beds populated with
herbs, vegetables, fruit, flowers, butterflies
and bees, is oval, since Robinson believed
that corners provided hiding-places for
animals. He would be glad that views of
the wooded rolling hills remain integral
to his influential English country garden.

Evening light lends romance to
Gravetye Manor. Here the house is
seen from the flower garden, which
is maintained in the style of William
Robinson, who owned Gravetye
for fifty-one years. Beds are filled
with a mixture of native and exotic
perennials, for Robinson disliked
formal beds planted annually with
flowers grown in greenhouses. He
also disapproved of parterres, but
championed a natural approach,
spurring on both cottage and
woodland gardening.

LEFT
A naturalistic scheme, where spires of pink digitalis, yellow verbascum and peach eremurus are striking verticals among eschscholzia, geranium and daisies.

BELOW
Mauve nepeta and irises complement the yellow *Cytisus battandieri* beside a path leading to a delicious rose- and wisteria-laden pergola.

OPPOSITE, TOP
The architecture at the back of the manor is obscured by a riot of mixed climbers and perennials: a triumph of informality.

OPPOSITE, BOTTOM
At one side of the house, a wild-flower meadow merges with the surrounding Sussex countryside.

43

Lady Farm
CHELWOOD, SOMERSET

Judy Pearce, who owns Lady Farm with her husband, Malcolm, could be described as a modern 'Capability' Brown. The scale of her achievement in transforming the landscape to create this garden is astounding. Formerly a farmer, she knew nothing about gardening, and the boldness of her concept was extraordinary. 'I brought a field down here', she says casually, indicating the topsoil she used to make a lawn and beds that replaced a concrete paddock surrounding the house. Next, the accidental discovery of a spring led to the creation of a landscaped watercourse spilling down a steep incline and finally sliding into two vast lakes. One is wilder in feel, one more clearly planted, but both are beautiful and expansive, with vistas beyond. Then, borrowing an idea she saw in Spain, Judy made a steppe garden: yellow, bronze and grey-mounded plants are interspersed with spires and spikes erupting from gravel and rocks. A prairie garden was added, with drifts of grasses and perennials. 'I get easily bored', admits Judy, in her garden of huge variety, where each area flows.

RIGHT
The cottage garden is seen through an arch of the summer house. Bold colours combine in the purple *Verbena bonariensis*, with scarlet *Persicaria amplexicaulis* 'Firetail' and wispy *Miscanthus sinensis* towards the back.

OPPOSITE, TOP
The circular thatched summer house is echoed by circular box hedging. The scheme of pink and purple includes mauve *Campanula lactiflora* 'Prichard's Variety', with *Rosa* 'Ballerina' and *R.* 'The Fairy'.

OPPOSITE, BOTTOM
Horticulture and nature merge. Some traditional garden plants, such as *Crocosmia* 'Lucifer' and *Alchemilla mollis*, are used throughout the garden, combined with such grasses as the stripy *Miscanthus sinensis* 'Strictus' — popular now, but an innovative choice at the time of the garden's creation.

LEFT AND OPPOSITE, TOP
Judy says: 'I made the lakes to get rid of excess water on the land, and planted to get rid of docks and nettles. I'd love to be a digger driver. You could change a whole scene in a day.' Now this lake looks as though it has always been there. Evening sun catches seed heads, embellishing the gold and bronze massed plantings of feathery *Stipa gigantea* and *S. tenuifolia*, umbels of achillea, red-hot pokers and the yellow towers of verbascum.

OPPOSITE, BOTTOM
The path to the lake runs through rhythmical plantings of perennials and grasses in yellow and orange. As Judy points out, 'These are good colours to be seen from a distance, where pastel shades disappear.'

44

The Old Zoo

BROCKHALL VILLAGE, LANCASHIRE

The Old Zoo garden was certainly the dream of its creator, the entrepreneur Gerald Hitman, who died in 2009. At 6 ft 5 in. Hitman was a larger-than-life character, with a garden to match. In 1992 he built a Modernist house on the site of a psychiatric hospital's petting zoo – hence the name. In 2000 he started work on the garden, with no masterplan. His son Harry says: 'First it was just piles of earth, and my dad stood out there conducting an orchestra of machines. As it took shape, it turned into something absolutely beautiful.' Gerald took advice from his young estate manager, David Smith, and designer Keith Pullan, but his own enthusiasm, determination and vision were crucial. With pleasure as its aim, the Old Zoo incorporates sensational use of water, an earthwork, two mazes, a hot tub, a croquet lawn and more than 100 dramatic sculptures. As for its future, Harry is philosophical: 'I think when the purchaser realizes the cost of upkeep, he will pick his favourite part, and the garden will evolve, becoming not only an expression of my father's creativity, but of his, too.'

RIGHT
Two bronze children form part of the largest private collection of the work of the Czech Republic's foremost sculptor, Olbram Zoubek. He became friends with Hitman after they met on holiday.

OPPOSITE, TOP
A stream with waterfall running through the garden is crossed by bridges, including this green-oak one by Derek Goffin.

OPPOSITE, BOTTOM
The Croquet Shelter, made from green oak by Derek Goffin, stands beside a frosty lawn, with the tawny winter tones of *Calamagrostis* × *acutiflora* 'Karl Foerster'.

A long rill cuts through the lawn beside the house and terrace, spilling from a pond with a sphere fountain. To the north is an excavated spiral, its slopes partly covered by cotoneaster, euonymus and potentilla.

OPPOSITE, BOTTOM
Morning sun brightens steps through woodland, beside the green-oak *Lake Shelter*, another inspiring work by Derek Goffin, with its roof of sedum and oak shingle. In front is a sculpture of a woman by Olbram Zoubek.

ABOVE
Joanna Mallin-Davies's *Brockhall Warrior* is set against the panorama of the Ribble Valley.

RIGHT
The playful mood of *The Tumbler* by Danny Clahane contrasts with a trio of mythological Bohemian princesses in painted concrete by Olbram Zoubek.

FAR RIGHT
An outdoor chapel contains a crucifix by Colin Mallett. Hitman allowed various artists to use the old hospital laundry as a studio, and to live in a nurses' accommodation block. He took sculptures in lieu of rent.

45

Cholmondeley Castle

MALPAS, CHESHIRE

Castles often have an air of intrigue and romance, and Cholmondeley, although built only in the nineteenth century, is no exception. Surrounded by sweeping, bulb-studded lawns and mature trees, and perched on a hill, it has panoramic views over a lake and cricket pitch. In the rose garden, rambling, tumbling roses and honeysuckle are underplanted with lavender in a profusion of pink and mauve – not a unique combination, but a winning one. It is the woodland and water gardens, however, that are the most enchanting. Acid-loving trees and shrubs thrive, and there are magnificent displays of rhododendrons, camellias and azaleas, as well as dogwood and magnolia. In spring a pocket-handkerchief tree (*Davidia involucrata*) is surrounded by white narcissus and bluebells. Finally, the Temple Garden, with its islands in a lake, its bridges and waterfalls, its twisted cedars and tiered pines, is like a Chinese painting that has come to life.

RIGHT AND OPPOSITE, TOP
Looking over the pond, the view widens out to lawns with layer upon layer of magnificent trees, including oaks, chestnuts, limes and weeping willows. The formal rill and lily pond are reached via a terrace beside the mock-Gothic castle, built in 1801.

OPPOSITE, BOTTOM
In the Temple Garden, a rustic bridge leads to an island in a small lake, where Koi carp swim lazily. The varied tree species beyond provide structure and colour throughout the year.

OPPOSITE
The green of the leaves on mature trees in late spring tempers the vivid colours of the rhododendrons.

LEFT AND BELOW
The mixture of heights, textures and blazes of colour along the woodland walk creates horticultural fireworks.

46

Pannells Ash Farm West

SUDBURY, SUFFOLK

This is essentially a garden for children. But since it is the garden of Marcus Harpur, it is also influenced by many of the gardens he has photographed, and displays a keen awareness of structure and composition, making it alluring in both winter and summer. A large lawn for children's play links the two main features: an ornamental and a vegetable garden. After seeing Piet Oudolf's Millennium Garden at Pensthorpe in Norfolk, Marcus and his wife, Mary, were inspired to create an area of dreamy drifts of tall perennials mingled with grasses. They are planted in two blocks, with a path snaking through the centre of each – almost like a sheep track – so one can walk among the plants. The vegetable garden, on the far side, is edged with wavy willow hurdles supporting espaliered fruit. The beds are arranged in a grid, and the children have their own plots and use their own tools. Millie grows currants, brassicas, nigella and lavender. Rupert likes edible flowers and gnomes.

A swing hangs from a branch of a walnut tree (*Juglans regia*), providing a strong silhouette in winter. When the family came to this house in 2001, the garden was split in two by a ditch, which is now fenced off for the safety of the children.

OPPOSITE
This garden, with its mounds of different textures, delicate grasses (including feathery *Stipa gigantea*) and seed heads, looks as good in winter as it does in summer, when dexterously packed poppies, alliums and aquilegia are flowering.

ABOVE
The unusual woven willow fence surrounding the vegetable garden is attractive but also functional: it creates a microclimate for the vegetables and cutting garden within.

LEFT
Paths lead through the ornamental garden, where in all seasons, grasses sway and shine.

169

47

Durand Garden

LONDON

This imposing 33.5 by 13.5-metre
(110 by 44-ft) town garden was intended
by its designer, Judith Sharpe, to be crisply
formal with some blowsiness in the borders.
She knew her client was quite a formal
person, but the brief was very open. Her
client had fallen in love with the box-head
pleached hornbeams Judith had used in
another garden, and so they became the
main feature. A generous patio for outdoor
dining was dug out on a lower level, reached
by French windows from the conservatory.
Mature pleached hornbeams form an axis
between the middle of the conservatory and
an arbour surrounded by rhododendrons,
camellias and maples. A huge bay tree that
once obscured the whole of the back of the
house now stands cloud-pruned, light and
lovely. The garden is tranquil because it is
not visually busy. Judith explains: 'The most
important aspect of garden design is the
division of space; the ratio of mass to void
is perfect here.'

RIGHT, TOP
In the border *Yucca gloriosa* 'Variegata',
Bergenia 'Bressingham White', *Cotinus
coggygria* 'Royal Purple', *Heuchera*
'Plum Pudding' and *Acanthus spinosus*
are planted with alliums and nepeta.
Threads of maroon and plum
flowers and foliage run through
the beds, for Judith believes these
colours give depth. They also go
well both with soft pastels and with
bolder oranges and lime greens.

RIGHT, BOTTOM
A ceramic dish by Stolzman and
Thomas is used as a birdbath, with
Primula vialii and the young foliage
of lavender and yew.

OPPOSITE, LEFT, FROM TOP
Papaver orientale 'Perry's White';
Osteospermum sp.; *Iris pallida*
'Variegata'; *Yucca gloriosa* 'Variegata'
with *Rosa* 'Buff Beauty'.

OPPOSITE, RIGHT
An avenue of pleached hornbeams
frames the view to a shady arbour.
As the sun comes over the garden,
blocks of shadow appear on the
grass, giving added drama.

48

Walsingham Abbey

NORFOLK

The medieval village of Little Walsingham
has been a place of pilgrimage since the
eleventh century. Two pillars made of flint
and stone either side of a pointed arch
containing the tracery of a window are
all that remains of the Augustinian abbey;
the rest has been replaced by an expanse
of daisy-sprinkled grass. But the abbey
grounds also include understated gardens
and, over an ancient packhorse bridge,
a river and unspoiled woodland walks.
They are outstanding in February, when
the riverbanks and woods are carpeted with
a heart-stopping display of naturalized
snowdrops. In summer the gardens hold
other pleasures. Set around the lawn are
a sunken garden, formed from more ruins,
with foxgloves sprouting from crevices and
roses planted between, and a well garden
with ferns and yew hedges. At the base of
each pillar of the ruined abbey is a small,
round bed of roses, lavender, peonies and
delphiniums, like a pool, enhancing rather
than detracting from the noble serenity.

The ruined abbey, glimpsed through
winter branches, is reflected in the
River Stiffkey. Snowdrops mingle
with the burgeoning spikes of
narcissi, the cheerful yellow flowers
of *Eranthis hyemalis* and the foliage of
ivy on the woodland floor.

LEFT
Thousands of clumps of *Galanthus nivalis* shine against a thick layer of fallen leaves.

OPPOSITE, TOP
The medieval packhorse bridge was originally outside the priory wall, on the main road to Norwich. In the nineteenth century the wall was moved outwards, to include the bridge as a feature of the landscaped garden.

OPPOSITE, BOTTOM
The sinuous, snaking outline of the River Stiffkey, flowing through the abbey grounds, is highlighted by the white flowers of the snowdrops on its banks.

49

East Wing, Thorp Arch Hall

WETHERBY, WEST YORKSHIRE

This gorgeous garden, developed since 1996 by its owners, Chris Royffe (a landscape architect) and his wife, Fiona, is a celebration of traditional English country style with a modern twist. A striking modernist courtyard with beech hedges and box cubes provides a geometric reference to the air vents in the stable building. A sculptural ha-ha of large diagonal stones creates an axis from a pond to a border hedge with holes cut out to take advantage of views of the parkland. There are also ponds and a potager. Planting is restrained, so that green dominates, although a particular colour in one area might appear in the next, linking the two. Because the garden is relatively small, areas of different character and atmosphere are delineated by high pleached screens rather than enclosing hedges or walls. Formality meets informality, as clipped shapes are minimalist rather than intricate in this inspirational garden for all seasons.

RIGHT
Wire chickens add a modern touch to the lawn beside the Royffes' home, which was once the coach house, stables and butler's quarters of Thorp Arch Hall, designed by John Carr in the 1750s. Trees (such as the overhanging weeping ash) planted at various times through the centuries form a backdrop to the garden, which has undergone big changes under its current owners.

OPPOSITE, TOP
The garden, which is just 0.3 hectares (¾ acre), wraps around the East Wing. A large oval clipped yew tree (one of the oldest trees in the garden) stands in the corner, and a splash of colour is provided by crocosmia.

OPPOSITE, BOTTOM
Variegated holly standards line a rectangle of hoggin (a traditional compacted surface) for boules.

ABOVE
In the gravel of the dry garden are beautifully clipped pine and yew. Hornbeams on the right are underplanted with soft mounds of pink *Geranium palmatum*.

RIGHT
A pencil-thin fountain gives a delicate feel and sound to a shady pond. Over the bridge, a grassy path leads between yew hedges that hide the treats to come.

FAR RIGHT
A serpentine hedge, dramatically cut into a zigzag, leads the eye towards a potager of productive plants and flowers for cutting, including kniphofia, dahlias and verbena.

OPPOSITE, TOP
A metallic half-cylinder fountain sculpture responds to the curve of the raised pond, providing relaxing background sound for the seating area.

OPPOSITE, BOTTOM
Yew cushions shelter under a pleached hornbeam hedge, which provides a visual screen as well as protection from north-easterly winds. Holes cut into the hornbeams allow glimpses out to the open land beyond.

50

Rousham

OXFORDSHIRE

The prevailing colour at Rousham is green. Green of every hue is seen in the grass, shrubs, trees and surrounding countryside beyond the River Cherwell, which forms an important backdrop to this exceptional garden. Designed by William Kent (c. 1685–1748), a hugely influential painter and architect, the garden represents one of the earliest and best examples of the English landscape tradition. Miraculously, it remains almost unaltered, retaining the serpentine rill, ponds, statues, temples and ruins that first delighted its eighteenth-century visitors. Still today, when you walk round Kent's intended route, scenes open up like stage sets, and yet tranquillity and naturalism are retained. Within the grounds, but a century older, is the walled garden with its box parterre and circular pigeon house. Fruit trees grown in every shape and form against the local honey-coloured stone are inspirational.

RIGHT, TOP
The walled garden next to the house was happily not demolished when Kent designed the park, and is an attraction in its own right, with exuberant borders spilling over box edging.

RIGHT, BOTTOM
A plain archway increases the surprise within, where foxgloves, roses and lavender jumble together.

OPPOSITE
A striking combination of lychnis, phlox, nepeta and echinacea in rich pinks and mauves provides a contrast of style and pace with the garden outside the walls.

LEFT
Cow Castle by William Kent: even
the cattle in the parkland were given
a picturesque shed.

BELOW
The River Cherwell with morning-
frosted grass and ethereal trees forms
one picture in the open-air gallery of
living landscapes that is Rousham.

OPPOSITE, TOP LEFT
A long serpentine rill winds down a
path towards the Temple of Echo.

OPPOSITE, TOP RIGHT
Horace Walpole wrote in 1760 that
Rousham possessed 'the sweetest little
groves, streams, glades, porticos,
cascades and river imaginable'. That
still applies: this is the lower cascade.

OPPOSITE, BOTTOM
An 'eyecatcher' statue of Apollo turns
his back on the Long Walk, framed
by trees on a cold autumn morning.

51

Colesbourne Park

CHELTENHAM, GLOUCESTERSHIRE

Colesbourne is galanthophile heaven: more than 160 varieties of snowdrop can be found there in vast swathes and drifts. But it also holds other delights, and other flowers, especially daffodils, crocuses, fritillaries and hellebores. Flowers sparkle in the extensive wood, in the Spring Garden, and by the lake and the river. In contrast to these gentle, natural settings are a formal garden and an intimate courtyard garden, where different snowdrops can be identified at close quarters, while beyond a rose pergola, irises and tulips prolong the display. Colesbourne was inherited by Henry Elwes, great-grandson of Henry John Elwes, who started the snowdrop collection and introduced the outstanding *Galanthus elwesii* in 1874. For almost a century the garden was neglected, until the younger Henry's wife, Carolyn, in true galanthophile fashion, gradually became obsessed. With the recent help of plantsman and writer John Grimshaw, she has made the collection one of the most significant, comprehensive and beautiful in the country.

RIGHT, CLOCKWISE FROM TOP
Galanthus 'S. Arnott' in drifts under trees; crocuses and *G. elwesii*; two portraits of *G. nivalis*; *Eranthis hyemalis*.

OPPOSITE, TOP
The Colesbourne estate comprises 1010 hectares (2500 acres), including four farms, 364 hectares (900 acres) of forest, most of the property in the village and this church.

OPPOSITE, BOTTOM
Winter branches are softened with a tactile coat of moss and ferns.

52

The Old Vicarage

WHIXLEY, NORTH YORKSHIRE

When Mr and Mrs Marshall arrived at the
vicarage in the late 1960s, the large trees in
the graveyard next door contributed shade
and seclusion, but the garden had no walls,
terraces or paths to give structure in winter.
Drawing inspiration from Sybil Spencer
at York Gate garden near Leeds, who said,
'Plants like to know where they are. You have
to give them a safe haven', Mrs Marshall
chose local materials, such as gravel and York
pavers, for hard landscaping. All the windows
of the vicarage look out over vistas, because
the garden is ingeniously engineered to
complement the house, which sits in the
middle. Near it are shades of cream, buff,
soft yellow and white; pink is avoided
against the red-brick walls. Favourite plants
are hellebores, roses, peonies and herbaceous
clematis in pastel shades; bright yellow, orange
and red are barred, because, as Mrs Marshall
explains, 'they don't suit this mellow garden'.

RIGHT
An assortment of terracotta
pots holds striking black *Aeonium*
'Zwartkop', pelargoniums, fuchsia,
verbena, marguerite and petunias.

OPPOSITE, TOP
A deep border is filled with lupins,
allium, peonies, achillea and nepeta.
Height is provided by an arch covered
in pale *Rosa* 'Moonlight', with peachy
R. 'Souvenir de la Malmaison' in
front. Over the door of the house is
pink *R.* 'May Queen', and scrambling
up the wall is – rather appropriately
– white *R.* 'Rambling Rector'.

OPPOSITE, BOTTOM
A gravel path runs like a river
towards the gazebo. On the left
are tall pink and white self-seeded
foxgloves, and on the right *Euonymus
fortunei* 'Emerald 'n' Gold'.

BELOW, FROM TOP
Salvia × sylvestris 'Mainacht' with love-in-a-mist (*Nigella damascena*); *Rosa* 'Mary Rose' and *Geranium palmatum*.

RIGHT
The view from the front of the house to the church includes box cones that echo the shape of the Gothic arch. In front are the indigo spires of *Salvia × sylvestris* 'Mainacht' and paler love-in-a-mist, with pink *Geranium palmatum* towards the back.

53

The Old Rectory

NORFOLK

Both exuberance and attention to detail reflect the character of the owner of this garden: a glasshouse has specially designed hinges; cold frames are made of bespoke curved aluminium, to resemble wood; and even bamboo canes are painted blue to match the trellis and furniture in the conservatory. Consideration has been given throughout to form and structural definition, resulting in an expanse of horticultural art that is as satisfying in winter as it is in summer. The garden was designed by the owner, who planted 4500 native deciduous and evergreen trees (as well as *Rhododendron ponticum*, to remind him of his childhood home), some to create privacy, and more to form a wood, traversed by narrow, winding paths. He installed a camellia house with a specially designed roof to stop rain spoiling the flowers of the potted camellias below. Through this summer house one enters another world: a walled garden with rectangular pond and herbaceous borders in peaceful straight lines. The intricate rose garden and the tranquil open fields beyond, by the lake, provide a contrast. Tender care, as well as hard work, has been lavished everywhere.

The rose garden, surrounded by beech and yew hedges, consists of a thigh-high box parterre (designed by the owner and a friend during a train journey to London) around an eighteenth-century Spanish clay oil jar. In summer intoxicating roses in pink and white are allowed to grow quite tall. In winter the geometric design becomes the principal player. Evergreens are 'the bones of the garden', says the owner, while deciduous trees 'fluff up the effect'.

54

Kirtling Tower

NEWMARKET, CAMBRIDGESHIRE

Rivers of blue flowers imprint themselves on the memory at the home of Lord and Lady Fairhaven. It is Lady Fairhaven's favourite colour, and when her son Rupert died of malaria, a field was planted with 6000 glorious camassias in his memory. Running the length of the moat at the back of the house is a carpet of 24,000 muscari and chionodoxa. Richard Ayres, head gardener at Anglesey (the Fairhavens' former home), designed and planted the gardens at Kirtling Tower. He delights in the walled garden, with its herbaceous borders and Tudor walk, planted with narcissi and tulips of the period. Another effective idea of his was to surround a hedge of elaeagnus, bordering the circular millennium garden, with a slightly higher one of copper beech, creating a bronze frame. One innovation, however, was copied from Lord Fairhaven. One morning at Anglesey, he was seen scrubbing the bark of silver birches with soap and water. The practice has been continued at Kirtling by the gardeners, with brilliant results.

Kirtling Tower (left) was built in the 1530s as the gatehouse to a hall that no longer exists. Beside it are Place Farm (where the Fairhavens' daughter lives) and an office (right). Old varieties of apple have been planted in Rupert's Garden, a field of camassias and pheasant's-eye narcissi (*Narcissus poeticus*).

RIGHT
When Richard Ayres told Lady Fairhaven about the camassias he had seen at Highgrove, she asked how many there were. He replied, 'About 300', to which she responded, 'Then we will have 3000.' That number has since doubled, making a spectacular sight in spring.

FAR RIGHT
Amazingly, this ancient oak grows out of a moat that borders Kirtling Tower on three sides.

BELOW
A mown path runs through the field of camassias beneath a vast oak tree, *Quercus robur*.

55

Chiffchaffs

GILLINGHAM, DORSET

This quintessential English cottage garden, with the added bonus of woodland, was lovingly developed from scratch. Ken and Gudrun Potts have owned the 400-year-old cottage, its surrounding garden and the adjoining nursery for thirty-one years. Gudrun was secretary to Graham Stuart Thomas; Ken worked for the Kent forestry commission, and during the war he would cycle past Sissinghurst, where he saw, but was too shy to talk to, Vita Sackville-West. Her influence, nevertheless, seems to have rubbed off: Chiffchaffs' sloping garden is cleverly divided into intimate 'rooms' at different levels, reached by narrow limestone paths affording glimpses of open countryside. Beds are packed with spring bulbs, herbaceous plants, annuals, old roses, rhododendrons and clematis for a long season of colour, and three-quarters of the propagating is done on site. The woodland garden includes ornamental trees, shrubs and a bog garden, and eighteen different species of *Liquidambar* have just been planted in this ever-evolving garden. 'It is a dream come true', smiles Mr Potts, sharing the personal charm created here.

RIGHT
Beside stone-and-gravel steps, dwarf heathers, rosemary, juniper, violas and berberis form a patchwork of colour in an alpine scree.

OPPOSITE, TOP
Cheerful cottage-garden borders front the stone house. Generous clumps of dahlia, helenium, anthemis, phlox, asters and nicotiana spill over the path in a profusion of colour.

OPPOSITE, BOTTOM
At the side of the house, a yew arch entices visitors to another part of the garden. Narcissi are planted between heathers and conifers on either side of the path, which is just part of the 8 cubic metres (283 cu. ft) of limestone brought into the garden.

56

Kensington Road

BRISTOL

The tiny inner-city courtyard garden of Alan Elms and Grenville Johnson is like a treasure trove, and the experience of visiting is filled with theatre, surprises and the infectious enthusiasm of the owners. A clue to the garden is given inside the Victorian terraced house, carefully packed with antiques; but one is whisked outside to a door in the wall to enter the garden, with the desired show-stopping effect. The plot, a mere 5.5 by 6 metres (18 by 20 ft), on two decked levels, includes seating, an Italianate garden, statuary, a stumpery inspired by Highgrove, a grotto and pond – all enveloping you at different stages. Everything is in pots, allowing density and versatility. Another trick is the use of large plants, giving illusions of the perimeter. What was once a lean-to with a privy, then a carport, is now a haven. 'The process has taken us on a magical journey,' says Grenville. Visitors share the magic, and learn that no space is too small for a fabulous garden.

RIGHT
Pip, the bronze hobgoblin, by Julian Jeffrey, plays in the woodland garden among ferns, agapanthus and impatiens. Perennials, summer bedding and evergreens give year-round interest, but all are planted in pots. The garden takes more than an hour to water, and in summer, it is done twice daily.

OPPOSITE, TOP
A bust of Brutus overlooks the Southern Hemisphere and Exotic Garden, inspired by Christopher Lloyd. Grenville jokes, 'I would like this garden to become a Little Dixter.' Clipped box mingles with tree ferns, *Cordyline australis*, the rhubarb-like leaves of *Gunnera manicata*, red-stemmed *Beschorneria septentrionalis* and *Fatsia japonica*, all planted in containers. On the table is yellow sedum.

OPPOSITE, BOTTOM
An urn and windchime add individuality.

57

Sheephouse

PAINSWICK, GLOUCESTERSHIRE

Sheephouse is neither so large as to be daunting, nor so grand as to be intimidating: it is a gentle garden in which to feel comfortable. Behind the house is a pond on two levels, a potager and lawns, which in spring deliver a generous show of bulbs. The whole is unified by a restricted colour palette (often derived from trees) and the use of stone, gravel and circles. A grey oak gazebo overlooks the pond, with a silver oak tree on one side and a silver-leaved weeping pear, *Pyrus salicifolia* 'Pendula', on the other. The lower level of the pond, semicircular and covered with duckweed, almost merges with the lawn in an emerald curve. Beyond the lawns and handsome trees are fields and rolling hills. Near the potager, a copper beech tree stands beside a hedge of the same species. The new shoots in the hedge glow red like sparks against the darker leaves of the tree, which turn in the wind, revealing purplish-green undersides to their almost black tops.

The Georgian part of the house, built of Painswick stone, can be seen at the side of the potager, its colour blending with the five-pointed gravel star and the stone urn holding petunias. Low box, culminating in cones, edges the five beds. Height and variety are provided by standard 'Iceberg' roses at the apex of each bed, while at the other end an arch bears apples or pears. A wigwam of canes supports beans and peas, with salad crops in the foreground.

OPPOSITE, TOP
The beech hedge on the left enfolds the garden, and on a misty morning, the fields beyond the boundaries gain an air of mystery and calm.

OPPOSITE, BOTTOM
A view from the gazebo shows *The Little Dancer*, found in a reclamation yard, now posing in a brick-edged circle in the pond.

LEFT
A metal seat surrounds a copper beech. Some 3500 bulbs have been planted here: snowdrops, crocuses and narcissi. It is often suggested that gardeners should throw bulbs and plant them where they fall, for a naturalistic effect, but here, narcissi have been carefully placed in rivers and sweeping swathes of sumptuous impact.

58

Hillwatering

BURY ST EDMUNDS, SUFFOLK

This is one of the most beautiful gardens. It relies on shape, texture and shades of green, rather than flowers, for it belongs to Jorn Langberg, former managing director of Dior, who dislikes colour. The garden fits the cottage it surrounds as a well-cut garment fits its wearer. 'A series of rooms' — that over-used phrase — is appropriate here. One enclosure suggests a grass rug on a gravel floor and box skirting around yew walls, with a white seat beside a standard lamp of white hibiscus. The herb garden, with carved box, a central olive and a rosemary arbour, provides every variety and texture of green and grey. Behind the house the garden opens to a wonderful pond, curved on the far side but approached by triangles of brick terracing that echo the apex of the thatched roof. Over a grey-painted bridge the planting is wilder. To the side, pleached hornbeams lead to a barn wall. A square window with a white frame holds a view of fields — a breathtaking picture incorporated into the garden. Exhibitions of sculpture are held annually here, but in the unadorned garden, serenity sings out.

RIGHT
The different levels, textures and shades of curving hedges give the impression of waves reaching shore.

OPPOSITE, TOP
A herringbone brick path complements the seventeenth-century terracotta-painted house, hugged by box balls and cones and *Euonymus fortunei* 'Emerald 'n' Gold'. A yew arch invites further exploration of this garden's rare achievement of intimacy and openness, formality and prettiness.

OPPOSITE, BOTTOM
The immaculate yew hedging, undulating like the folds and flow of skirt-hems, is seen from the balcony of the studio. *Pyrus salicifolia* 'Pendula' adds a greyer green to the palette.

59

David Austin Roses

ALBRIGHTON, WEST MIDLANDS

The rose is one of the nation's best-loved flowers, and David Austin – although modest and shy – is one of the world's foremost rose experts. He has hybridized and grown roses for more than forty years: he introduced the uniquely charming 'English' rose and has created one of the best rose gardens in the world at his nursery near Wolverhampton. The garden consists of five themed areas with more than 700 different varieties of rose, whether shrubs and standards in beds, or climbers and ramblers supported against walls or scrambling over pergolas, arches and arbours. Formal yew hedges surround the gardens, and the roses displayed include hybrid teas, wild roses, modern and old roses and English roses. In the elegant Renaissance Garden a long rectangular pool reflects the blooms at its side; in the impressive Lion Garden, roses mingle with herbaceous perennials. Throughout are sculptures by David's wife, Pat Austin, in settings of intoxicating colour and scent.

RIGHT
Pink *Rosa* 'Gertrude Jekyll' is tall and vigorous with a particularly strong old-rose fragrance. It can also be grown as a short climber. Here, it appears with *R.* 'Wenlock', a shorter, crimson variety.

OPPOSITE, TOP, FROM LEFT
'Abraham Darby' is a shrub rose with deeply cupped blooms in shades of pink, apricot and yellow, produced continuously; 'Madame Grégoire Staechelin' is a climber with semi-double, pink flowers with a sweet-pea fragrance; 'Claire Jacquier', a tall peach-coloured climber with a delicious fragrance, flowers once a season.

OPPOSITE, BOTTOM
Most notable in this garden are the English roses, introduced by David Austin. These combine the form and scent of old roses with the wide colour range and repeat flowering of modern roses. They are shrubs, but can be grown as standards and climbers, especially on arches and pergolas, since they reach a height of about 2.5 metres (8 ft).

60

Buscot Park

FARINGDON, OXFORDSHIRE

A tree-lined avenue leading to the Palladian house gives an indication of the grounds, which are grand and formal with long, straight paths cutting through grass. The walled garden is approached by a gravel path lined with Portuguese laurel clipped into *Alice in Wonderland* lollipops. Standard roses and lollipop-shaped verbascum add to the effect, until a classical fountain is reached. It is surrounded by pleached New Zealand hop hornbeam, also forming an avenue, strikingly underplanted with alliums. Steep steps bordered by blocks of yew lead towards the house. To the east, through woodland walks, is one of England's finest water gardens, designed by Harold Peto in 1904. Italianate formality blends with English parkland as a stone-edged canal crossed by a balustraded bridge runs into a series of pools of various shapes. The canal culminates in a vast lake, complete with temple on the far shore. Throughout the garden vistas entice: at the end of each avenue is a stone statue, wrought-iron gate, marble vase or terracotta urn.

RIGHT
Harold Peto was the leading exponent of formal Italianate garden style in his day. His canal runs over narrow rills, miniature cascades and under bridges, flanked by box and cyprus hedges sheltering statues and jars. It is a triumph of variety and drama within form.

OPPOSITE
Peto was employed to improve the link between the house and the lake. He created a phenomenal chain of stairways, paths, basins and canals, on a terraced slope. From the top, the bold axis, which follows an earlier Victorian arboretum, is clearly seen.

An intersected avenue of pleached *Ostrya carpinifolia* (hop hornbeam) provides a strong vista.

FAR LEFT
Throughout Buscot, views, perspectives, focal points and straight lines provide an architectural structure of masterful elegance.

LEFT
Robinia pseudoacacia 'Frisia' combines strikingly with *Alchemilla mollis*, lysimachia, roses and nepeta.

BELOW
The mellow red-brick walls of the original kitchen garden now house the Four Seasons Garden, created by the present Lord Faringdon. Here, repeated plantings of lysimachia and nepeta add rhythm to wide borders.

61

Abbotsbury Subtropical Gardens

ABBOTSBURY, DORSET

Next to the archetypal English village of Abbotsbury, with its picturesque cottages, bed-and-breakfasts and teashops, are these exotic subtropical gardens. Established in 1765, they have developed into 8 hectares (20 acres) of plants from all over the world, discovered by generations of plant hunters. The mild maritime climate and protecting chalk-and-limestone hills enable the growth of the gardens' famed rare and colourful plants. Equally striking is the incredible variety in form and texture of foliage: from finger-like fronds to paddle-shaped leaves to veritable umbrellas. In the high canopy above, and on the dense floor below, are needles, straps, ovates, fans, peltates and more. Added to this are the wondrous textures and colours of bark, not to mention the flowers. The gardens include a spectacular hydrangea walk; ponds with lilies of every hue; a Victorian garden with a riot of fiery cannas, rudbeckias, dahlias and crocosmia; and a Mediterranean garden where drifts of blue agapanthus combine with dwarf aromatic *Lavandula dentate*.

RIGHT
Sun filters through the fan-shaped leaves of the Chusan palm (*Trachycarpus fortunei*).

OPPOSITE
Beside curving stone steps, the red–purple panicles bearing tubular red flowers of *Beschorneria yuccoides* are offset against the dark cork oak behind.

LEFT
Bold red-painted wooden bridges span the meandering stream. The lush vegetation, grown in the moist organic soil, includes tree ferns, variegated hostas, hydrangea and pink and yellow candelabra primulas, with the large leaves of gunnera towards the back.

BELOW
Colourful, spiky accents are provided by (from top) *Acanthus mollis*, *Kniphofia* 'Bees' Sunset' and *Francoa sonchifolia* Rogerson's form.

219

62

High Hall

IPSWICH, SUFFOLK

Trees contribute much that is celebratory
at High Hall, home since 1994 to sculptor
Maryanne Nicholls and her husband, Mark.
An orchard contains a 120-year-old apple
tree and several pear trees, proudly pruned
by Mark into skilful spreading shapes.
A 400-year old oak adds majesty to this
family garden of 3.6 hectares (9 acres),
which is developing gradually, and is used in
many ways. It accommodates wide areas of
grass, a croquet lawn, a naturalistic pond
and a swimming pool, as well as a buttercup
field, which becomes a car park and a stage
for productions of Gilbert and Sullivan
operas. Maryanne has a studio and holds art
classes in the garden, too. The more
ornamental areas are close to the house,
where plant combinations reflect an artist's
eye for colour and form. Cream verbascum
mingles with maroon circium in one corner,
purple–blue echium and lavender combine
with pink roses in another, and a white
sculpture is surrounded by cow parsley.

RIGHT, TOP
Under a mullioned window grows
Rosa 'Perle d'Or', a China rose with
pale apricot flowers, its darker buds
matching the colour of the old brick.

RIGHT AND FAR RIGHT
In the herbaceous border, spires of
foxgloves and verbascum contrast
with the white froth of *Crambe
cordifolia*; the doorway from the
back terrace to the old oak tree
is surrounded with jasmine.

OPPOSITE, TOP
The stone path at the front of the
house is bordered by box mounds,
adding a touch of formality to the
wild meadow in the orchard.

OPPOSITE, BOTTOM
The house, which dates from 1601,
may have been a hunting lodge
before becoming a farmhouse.
It was extended in the 1920s. Here,
philadelphus scents the garden
behind the house.

BELOW
A box circle contains *Vessel*, a
sculpture in steel and slate resin
by Maryanne Nicholls.

RIGHT
The 400-year-old oak was struck by
lightning in 2006, but despite a scar
in its trunk, it survived, magnificent
– more dramatic than before.

OPPOSITE, TOP
The setting sun disappears beyond
the oak tree.

OPPOSITE, BOTTOM
Evening sun shines on the mown
path through the meadow. An avenue
of hornbeams (*Carpinus betulus*
'Fastigiata') was planted in 2005.

64

Haddon Lake House

ST LAWRENCE, ISLE OF WIGHT

Just as one cannot appreciate light without dark, joy without sadness, so, too, the contrasts within this garden enrich the experience of the whole. The contemporary house appears to float on a lake, and a Japanese courtyard leads into a Victorian walled garden like no other. When Phillippa and Stephen Lambert bought the derelict site, a condition of the planning consent entailed restoring its Victorian features, dating from the 1820s. No records exist of the courtyard, so Phillippa, a landscape designer, was able to put her own imprint on it, although the Victorian owner, William Spindler, was so modern in his outlook that she feels he would have approved. Through the minimalist courtyard is the breathtaking walled garden with its gloriously robust plant combinations. The exceptional microclimate is maximized by Phillippa's planting of gutsy tropical borders. Her words are telling: 'The garden has a dream-like quality in that you cannot pin it down. You can look at any one part and you are never quite sure what country or what time you are in.'

RIGHT
Resin-bound gravel paths snake through tropical borders of canna, ginger, dahlia and self-sown echium. In front are violet *Verbena* 'Homestead Purple' and pale-pink *Diascia personata*.

OPPOSITE, TOP LEFT
This serene stone was found on site. Beside *Dicksonia antarctica* and *Phormium* 'Green Sword', a modest door in the cool, contemporary courtyard leads to the surprise sumptuous walled garden.

OPPOSITE, TOP RIGHT AND BOTTOM
In the walled garden, a period-style greenhouse, fruit, vegetables and flowers mingle joyously. *Dahlia* 'Bishop of Llandaff' contrasts with *Aster* × *frikartii* 'Mönch', with sweetcorn in front. Bold planting outside the walls includes cannas (*C. indica* 'Russian Red', *C. iridiflora* and 'Pretoria') and *Ricinus communis* 'Zanzibariensis'. The garden has been described by Laurence Llewelyn-Bowen as 'like an exploding Victorian sofa'.

ABOVE, LEFT
Tree ferns add accent to a shady
bank by the lake.

ABOVE, RIGHT
A stream leads from the boathouse
to the lake, planted with hostas,
carex, *Typha minima* and *Cornus alba*
(foreground), and ricinus, cannas
and *Salvia uliginosa* (behind).

LEFT
A wild, damp woodland area
dating from the 1820s completes
this many-faceted garden.

OPPOSITE
In front of the house, a gravity-
powered fountain adorns the
0.13-hectare (⅓-acre) lake, which
is fed by several springs.

65

Ripley Castle

HARROGATE, NORTH YORKSHIRE

The substantial and successfully restored walled gardens and pleasure grounds of Ripley Castle, home to the Ingilby family for 700 years, are steeped in history. In this typical old English estate, with its impressive lakes, long and spectacular herbaceous borders, kitchen garden and park with ancient trees (some a staggering 1000 years old), each feature has a quality of the unexpected or of something extra. The view across the ornamental lake is ennobled by its backdrop of the castle; fallow deer, cattle and pheasants enliven the park. In the Victorian kitchen garden are herbs and a collection of rare vegetables grown in association with the Henry Doubleday Research Association (or Garden Organic). Moreover, the Grade II-listed greenhouses contain unusual collections of tropical plants, ferns and cacti, and Ripley Castle also holds the National Collection of hyacinths.

RIGHT
The crenellated castle wall dramatically shelters naturalized pheasant's-eye narcissi (*N. poeticus*).

OPPOSITE, TOP
The white and green shades of viridiflora tulip 'Spring Green' subtly harmonize with the grass and narcissi against the left wall.

OPPOSITE, BOTTOM
The Amcotts family, which is associated with Ripley Castle, has as its crest a squirrel, formed here from box topiary and *Myosotis sylvatica* 'Ultramarine'.

233

66

Hever Castle

EDENBRIDGE, KENT

The most striking features of the gardens at Hever Castle, laid out between 1904 and 1908, are the Italianate Garden, the moat and the water features. The whole benefits from views of the stately childhood home of Anne Boleyn. The meadow in front of the castle is golden with daffodils in spring, while Virginia creeper – which clads the castle walls – and such trees as Japanese maple and beech provide fabulous autumn colour. Neither is colour lacking in summer: the Italianate Garden is planted with spectacular roses and clematis as well as exuberant perennials and shrubs. It also houses William Waldorf Astor's collection of sculpture, and has at its far end a 14-hectare (35-acre) artificial lake. Throughout the year yew topiary stands majestically, dexterously forming a chess set and a maze, and providing a semicircular curtain against which classical statuary and a half-moon pond take spotlight position.

RIGHT, TOP
The grounds of the thirteenth-century castle are hidden here under a blanket of snow. The creation of the gardens employed 1000 men.

RIGHT, BOTTOM
An urn and evergreen trees add permanent elegance to this garden for all seasons.

OPPOSITE
A snow carpet leads to the lake under a magnificent stone pergola, bearing the winter branches of roses, wisteria and crab apple.

67

Trebah Garden

FALMOUTH, CORNWALL

The site of this 11-hectare (28-acre) subtropical parkland garden was first mentioned in the Domesday Book. Trebah, with its stream and ponds, became a famous pleasure garden in the nineteenth century, but by the time the property was sold in 1981 the garden was lost beneath forty years' neglect. It has now been spectacularly restored, with stunning views over rhododendrons, tree ferns and bamboos to a ravine and the Helford River. Huge, primeval, architectural plants amaze the eye, while the sound of cascading water assails the ears. In summer more than 0.8 hectares (2 acres) of massed blue and white hydrangea pour down the sides of the valley. Plants and trees from all over the world are found in this garden, some rarely seen growing in the open in England. Their names alone conjure the exotic: bottlebrush, Brazilian spider flower and ginger lily are only three examples. Above all, and unusually in a garden open to the public, Trebah is still exhilaratingly wild.

RIGHT
Palms are just some of the trees that contribute to this plant-lovers' subtropical paradise.

OPPOSITE
The eighteenth-century house is seen beyond a border of hydrangea, echium, trachycarpus and cordyline.

236

ABOVE, LEFT
The pale fronds of tree fern
Dicksonia antarctica darken with age.

ABOVE, RIGHT
A stone-chip path leads through a
bog garden in the valley, where damp
planting thrives, sheltered by trees.
Here, most prominently, is astilbe,
with pink bergenia.

LEFT
Tree ferns, cordyline, Mexican daisies
and ivy create a shady setting for
a bench. Seats are important in this
steep garden, providing rest as well
as places from which to admire
foliage and scale.

OPPOSITE
Ferns add colour, texture and
drama to the pool: a symphony
of green. Despite appearances, a
heron above the waterfall actually
provides protection for the fish.

68

Barnards Farm

WEST HORNDON, ESSEX

This extraordinary 17-hectare (42-acre) garden was designed, in part, from the air. Its owner, Bernard Holmes, flies a Cessna, and is meticulous about position and precision. An axis runs from his desk in the conservatory, through a vast avenue of clipped leylandii and over a pond to *The Sitooterie* by Thomas Heatherwick. This aluminium cube summer house has more than 5000 long, thin rods projecting from each surface, lifting it off the ground. There are more than sixty sculptures in the garden, not all as fantastical, but all impressive. Moving and miraculous is a 1920s bicycle shop, exactly reproduced (outside and in) from a photo owned by Bernard's father, in whose memory it was created. The estate manager, Barry Dorling, acts like a genie, granting Bernard's wishes and whims. He has placed sculpture, planted 6000 trees (including the National Collection of *Malus*), made a belvedere and helped create the many moods of the garden. 'I am happy to work for someone demanding in Bernard's way', he says. 'Imagine what fun I have had trying to get it right.'

RIGHT
A hut stands in a wild-flower meadow, with electricity wires above. Pylons run across the garden and are used in remarkable ways. Beside the Japanese garden is a sculpture made from insulators, and a plinth holding a head by Elisabeth Frink is a miniature pylon, placed at the same angle as the wires above.

OPPOSITE
Grand Passeur by Nicolas Lavarennne stands over the pond in dreamy tranquillity. Several of Lavarenne's stunning bronze sculptures on poles (including a lookout and a pole vaulter) add drama to this garden.

OVERLEAF
A river runs through Bernard's farm, and at sunset the scene is mystical.

69

Goodnestone Park

WINGHAM, KENT

Stupidly arriving on a Monday, when this garden is closed, I spotted Lady FitzWalter leaving in her car. Seeing my crestfallen face, she said I could visit on my own. Thus I was able to imagine myself one of Jane Austen's heroines, strolling in the garden that once belonged to the novelist's brother (Austen wrote *Pride and Prejudice* immediately after staying here in 1796). The garden retains the original eighteenth-century park, but cleverly incorporates features that have been added in the intervening years. Behind the grand house, built in 1704, is a terraced lawn. Central steps lead to a lime avenue, with wild flowers growing under impressive oaks, cedars and chestnuts on each side. Beyond are an attractive pond and rock garden, and an arboretum and woodland with many acid-loving trees and shrubs. In the wonderful walled garden, old roses mingle with mixed underplanting and ancient walls are clad with clematis and jasmine, all overlooked by the twelfth-century flint tower of the parish church.

RIGHT
The garden has undergone several changes, from formal to landscape to disrepair and restoration. In front of the Palladian house, built by Brook Bridges, a broad flight of steps leads to a parterre, designed by Charlotte Molesworth to celebrate the millennium.

OPPOSITE, TOP
A glint through a gate is a prologue to the fabulous surprise awaiting the visitor who enters the walled garden.

OPPOSITE, BOTTOM
The walled area behind the house dates from the sixteenth and seventeenth centuries. Restored in the 1960s and 1970s, the walls are here hung with clematis and wisteria, as though with a lavish bedspread.

70

The Exotic Garden

NORWICH, NORFOLK

Will Giles, owner and designer of this East
Anglian garden, says, 'It is like a stage set.
It is almost out of place here, because I have
tried to create a garden that transports you to
somewhere else.' In that, he has triumphantly
succeeded; the garden envelops the visitor
with ever-changing vistas. At the age of seven
Will was taken to Kew by his grandmother,
and he still remembers entering the Palm
House. The smell, humidity and enormous
leaves fitted his fantasy world, igniting a
passion that still exists. Over the years he has
sought out plants that give the same effect,
but that are hardy and can grow outdoors. He
also uses tender exotics, which he overwinters
in polytunnels, to add fiery colour. The
planting is staggering, but the hard
landscaping also astounds. A large wooden
tree house nestles high in an old oak, while
sunken paths are walled with local flint.
Whether you lose yourself in tropical foliage,
or look up at desert cacti, the drama thrills.

RIGHT
The raised pond is home not only
to water lilies, but also to the lance-
shaped leaves of *Pontederia cordata*, a
marginal aquatic perennial from the
swamp ditches of South America.

OPPOSITE, TOP
The dramatic tree house, built on
stilts by the owner, measures 5 by
5 metres inside (16½ by 16½ ft), so
there is plenty of room for relaxing
or working.

OPPOSITE, BOTTOM
The house, in the middle of the
garden, is almost totally hidden by
creepers, while pots and containers
filled with exotic plants adorn the
porch and steps.

A different world is manifest from the tree house. 'I did it on a very tight budget, but tried to create a very grand effect', Will explains. 'I have had lots of unpaid help from people who see my vision and want to get hooked into it.'

OPPOSITE, BOTTOM
Texture, form and colour create an exotic composition. Here, the glaucous leaves of tall *Arundo donax*, the lance-like foliage of yucca and the fan-shaped Chusan palm (*Trachycarpus fortunei*) combine with the scarlet flowers of canna and the striking red leaves of persicaria.

RIGHT
Steps are formed from stone, railway sleepers and gravel. The Mediterranean atmosphere is achieved with a loggia of local flint, enhanced by the planting of xerophyllum.

FAR RIGHT
A headless statue – complete with pumpkin – in a stone archway makes a focal point.

BELOW
A gravel path through raised beds, in places 1.8 metres (6 ft) high, enables the visitor to look up at the cacti and succulents.

71

The Gibberd Garden

HARLOW, ESSEX

Sir Frederick Gibberd (1908–1984) was
the Modernist architect responsible for
Heathrow Airport's terminal buildings,
Liverpool's Metropolitan Cathedral and
Harlow New Town, among others. This
background is evident in this gently sloping
3-hectare (7-acre) garden, with its enclosed
areas of different size and character, and in
Gibberd's statement that 'garden design is an
art of space'. He moved here in 1956, but it
was after his second marriage, in 1972, that
sculpture in the garden increased from just
three pieces to eighty. Sir Frederick and Lady
Gibberd developed the garden as set designers
might create scenery, against which actors –
in this case, the sculptures – can better
stimulate and amuse. The visitor experiences
changes of pace from drama to tranquillity
with woodland glades, groves, streams
and pools, lawns and *allées*. They provide
perfect settings for modern sculptures,
pots and architectural salvage, as well as
a wooden moated castle for Sir Frederick's
grandchildren to play in.

RIGHT
In this Modernist garden, woodland
landscape is used as a stage for
sculpture as well as *objets trouvés*,
such as the classical Portland stone
pillars salvaged from Coutts Bank
when Sir Frederick remodelled it.

OPPOSITE, TOP LEFT
The canal, diffused by soft moss,
delicate irises and foamy *Alchemilla
mollis*, makes an inspirational
frame for the powerful stone fist
Not in Anger by Leon Underwood.

OPPOSITE, TOP RIGHT
Two dogs by Robert Clatworthy
run, lifelike, in the grass.

OPPOSITE, BOTTOM
Urns, also rescued from Coutts
Bank, emerge from a shady area
of ivy and acanthus.

252

72

Smallwood Farmhouse

BURY ST EDMUNDS, SUFFOLK

This informal country garden – airy and subtle – is clearly designed by accomplished owners. There is a pleasing balance of scale and proportion, with different areas of interest blending into a relaxed whole. An idyllic duck pond in front of the 500-year-old thatched house is flanked by a surprising gravel garden, stylish and contemporary with its black fencing and white climbers. In the centre is a metal sculpture of cow parsley, a clue to what lies ahead – for the real thing billows in the meadow beyond, glimpsed through a hole in the fence. Around the house are irregular beds unified by repetition of plants, while plumes of cotinus match the house paint. Old roses abound, climbing through every tree and up grey–blue supports. A small stream runs beside the house, where fritillaries and bee orchids thrive under crab apple, quince and mulberry. A seductive combination of nature and horticulture, elegance and romance, intimacy and expansiveness is achieved.

RIGHT, TOP
The Suffolk-pink house is made of clay from the duck pond, which is surrounded by irises, grasses and *Rosa* 'Blanche Double de Coubert'.

RIGHT, BOTTOM
A seat in the evening garden invites lingering beside highly scented planting: old roses, jasmine, honeysuckle and philadelphus.

OPPOSITE, TOP
At the back of the house, mown paths thread through an ancient meadow. Under the apple tree the long grass is strewn with ox-eye daisies (*Leucanthemum vulgare*).

OPPOSITE, BOTTOM
Hardy geraniums, poppies and white foxgloves are massed in front of the blue-painted pergola and trellis, which are graced by old roses, including *Rosa gallica* 'Versicolor', 'Souvenir du Docteur Jamain' and 'Ferdinand Pichard'.

73

Renishaw Hall

DERBYSHIRE

The lasting impression of Renishaw Hall is that of a formal Italian garden, which complements the imposing hall and creates a perfect balance with the adjacent ancient bluebell wood. Renishaw Hall has been the home of the fascinating Sitwell family for 400 years, and it was Sir George Sitwell (who spent much of his time in Italy) who laid out the classical Italian garden in 1895. It is one of the most beautiful in England. George's grandson, Sir Reresby Sitwell, and his wife, Lady Penelope, did much to restore the garden in the years before Sir Reresby's death in 2009. They retained the antique statues, terraces and columns and the clipped yew hedges and pyramids, while enlarging the borders. In summer the riot of roses and delphiniums, in particular, is sensational. All is accompanied by the sound of splashing water, for there is a stupendous water jet as well as still pools and a lake.

RIGHT
The imposing hall stands on a terrace, below which is a bed of *Asphodeline lutea*, producing fragrant yellow flowers in spring.

OPPOSITE, TOP
Clipped yew frames a statue of Neptune acquired by Sir George Sitwell on one of his many tours of Italy. He wrote: 'Statuary proclaiming the imaginative ideal may strike in the garden a keynote of wonder and romance.'

OPPOSITE, BOTTOM
To one side of the house, geometric yew topiary adds substance and drama, while two Italianate marble fountains resemble candles in their holders. In wet weather the Veronese marble turns from grey to pink.

OPPOSITE
Sir Hamo Thornycroft's statue
The Angel of Fame, regilded by Lady
Sitwell, is a focal point at the end
of a lime avenue on the top lawn.

ABOVE
A Gothic folly is almost subsumed by
the vegetation of the ancient wood.

RIGHT
In early May the bluebell wood is
carpeted in cobalt. Camellias and
other acid-loving trees and shrubs
add further colour and interest.

74

Langton Farm

NORTHALLERTON, NORTH YORKSHIRE

Awareness of light and a painterly approach
to planting make this 0.3-hectare (¾-acre)
village garden outstanding. Annabel Fife, who
lives here with her husband, asked her parents
for a greenhouse when she was ten years
old; she is now a garden designer. The site is
triangular, bordered on two sides by the River
Swale. 'Rooms' within include a romantic,
colour-themed octagonal flower garden; a
walnut garden with spring bulbs; and a bee
garden with drifts of thistles, perovskia and
limonium. Annabel's study of interior design
informs her use of space, as well as the effect
of light on colour. Pale, diffuse shades flower
in spring, when the sun is low; in summer
the garden is filled with hotter hues, because
the high sun burns out colour. The overall
composition is as important here as the
individual elements. A soft quality is
achieved with gauzy washes of colour, and
skilful pruning transforms blocks of plants
into more transparent shapes, layered one on
top of the other, as in a watercolour painting.

RIGHT
A path of handmade bricks leads
through the garage. Colour-themed
planting includes pale-blue *Ceanothus*
× *delileanus* 'Gloire de Versailles',
purple *Salvia horminum* spilling on to
the path, and the spires of *Verbascum
chaixii* 'Album' (white flowers with
mauve centres).

OPPOSITE, TOP
Borders in the octagonal garden start
with pastels and blues; pale yellows
then progress to orange, red, maroon,
hot pink and back to pale pink. All is
unified by foliage: in the foreground
we see the silver *Artemisia ludoviciana*
and the glaucous leaves of sedum.

OPPOSITE, BOTTOM
The red border displays Annabel's
masterly use of layers of colour. A
pleached red-twigged lime hedge is
planted behind pruned, purple-leaved
Cotinus 'Grace' (a translucent red
in autumn) and chocolate-leaved
sambucus. Centre stage is scarlet
Crocosmia 'Lucifer' with a fountain of
blue–grey *Melianthus major* beneath, to
cool the palette. Framing the view is
red-berried *Sorbus vilmorinii*.

OPPOSITE, TOP
The side of the house is seen
through a fiery haze of *Crocosmia*
'Lucifer' teamed with scarlet *Lychnis
chalcedonica* in the foreground, offset
against *Heuchera* 'Plum Pudding'.

OPPOSITE, BOTTOM
A shady green corridor, flanked
by a beech hedge and blocks of yew,
leads to the front of the house and
a huge walnut tree. This formal
walk, with its row of pleached
limes, counterbalances the billowy
octagonal garden on the other side.

ABOVE
A fountain bubbling from a round
stone in a pebble pool is surrounded
by box balls, sanguisorba and
lavender. Behind is an orange border.
A wooden bench sports orange
cushions, with a ledge on the wall
behind for candles, wine glasses and
scented geraniums. Beside the seat
are marigolds and orange crocosmia.

RIGHT
The golden hop (*Humulus lupulus*
'Aureus') swarms up attractive wooden
supports that form a tunnel in front
of the orange seat shown above.

75

Hodsock Priory

WORKSOP, NOTTINGHAMSHIRE

This atmospheric garden is famed for its displays of snowdrops (*Galanthus*), the harbingers of spring. There is a magical woodland walk through thousands of these delicate flowers, enhanced by the potent fragrance of sarcococca and winter honeysuckle, and the sight of the coloured stems of cornus and willow reflected in the lake. In this winter garden snowdrops spread through borders, grow in the grass under trees and mingle with magenta cyclamen and yellow winter aconites (*Eranthis hyemalis*). In its grounds of 2 hectares (5 acres), Hodsock also boasts two ferneries, beautiful banks dripping with hundreds of hellebores, and working Victorian beehives.

RIGHT, TOP
Narcissi, drooping slightly after a frosty night, make a golden ribbon along the banks of the stream.

RIGHT, BOTTOM
No garden need be dull in February. Here, a spectacular partnership of snowdrops, heather and hellebores forms a generous quilt.

OPPOSITE
Soft rays of winter sun light the brick priory, perfectly matching the dry leaves of the beech hedge, while thrusting branches echo the soaring chimneys.

Upturned sunny *Eranthis hyemalis*, modest nodding hellebores and young shoots of iris and narcissus under trees offer joy now and promised pleasure.

Snowdrops beneath witch hazel in the early spring – a delectable and fragrant pairing.

76

Saling Hall

BRAINTREE, ESSEX

Hugh Johnson, the writer on wine and gardens, owns this thought-provoking garden with its outstanding arboretum. A self-proclaimed collector of trees, he explains that he 'set out to evoke different moods and responses throughout the garden, from cheerful to solemn'. A walled garden behind the house is filled with plants anchored by topiary, its contained extravagance both pleasing and creating a compelling tension. A wilder section of the garden is reached through an iron gate: pillars and statues provide focal points, but the chief attraction is the huge variety of rare trees and shrubs, deliberately planted to display their varying heights, textures and multitude of greens. A dark, upright conifer is next to a bright, domed maple beside a splayed Judas tree. A path of mown grass through an avenue of immensely tall, straight oaks, culminating in an oak circle, is cathedral-like. Elsewhere, a pond with island, hammock and four white-trunked *Betula utilis* var. *jacquemontii* 'Jermyns' evokes a lighter mood. Exciting bark abounds: peeling red–brown *Acer griseum*, golden *Prunus maackii* and grey-and-peach *B. utilis* var. *jacquemontii*, like raw silk.

RIGHT
The autumnal gold of *Acer rubrum* is resplendent beside stone steps leading to the water garden.

OPPOSITE, TOP
A herringbone path (harmonizing with the walls and house) leads through the walled garden, which was laid out by the previous owner, Lady Carlyle, in 1946. Rectangular beds edged with low box are punctuated with Irish junipers interspersed with herbaceous plants, herbs and shrub roses in a largely pastel palette.

OPPOSITE, BOTTOM
In the centre of the walled garden is a mid-eighteenth-century statue of Flora, goddess of flowers, surrounded by a vine-draped octagonal iron pergola by Giuseppe Lund. Box pyramids frame the view.

ABOVE
Shafts of light, filtered patterns and shadows are important players in this garden, as here, where a fastigiate yew acts as a statuesque focal point.

RIGHT AND FAR RIGHT
Stone features provide elegance and a sense of permanence.

OPPOSITE
Bordering the Japanese garden, individually clipped box bushes huddle together to form a curvaceous cloud wall. They are reminiscent of evergreen azaleas, which are often similarly clipped in Japan but are too tender to grow in England.

78

Pashley Manor

WADHURST, EAST SUSSEX

The tulips here are renowned, but there is much else to appreciate, too. Keen attention has been paid to the seamless merging of the garden with both the house and the undulating countryside beyond. There is a permanent exhibition of modern sculpture, including some wonderful works by Philip Jackson, placed to enhance both garden and artworks. But especially noteworthy here is a subtle use of colour. A small courtyard is paved with brick and the planting against the house wall is stunning. Circular swirls of trained fig create an unusual tracery behind astonishing *Paeonia* × *lemoinei* 'Souvenir de Maxime Cornu', a tree peony with huge coral-and-cream flowers that harmonize perfectly with the faded terracotta-coloured brick. Following a long path towards distant sheep-dotted hills are other enclosed areas (with boundaries low enough to see the countryside beyond), gradually incorporating more grass, with colour-themed herbaceous planting. A kitchen garden, bluebell walk and large pond complete this sumptuous garden.

RIGHT
In November the ground is mulched with Pashley's own sheep manure, and around 15,000 tulip bulbs are planted for the tulip festival in April and May. Here, they make blocks of colour under an apple tree, edged with pansies.

OPPOSITE, TOP
Landscape architect Anthony du Gard Pasley helped with the renovation of the garden, which is now maintained by four full-time gardeners. Tulips in a mix of flamboyant colours uplift the spirits here; elsewhere swathes in one colour are planted for softer effect.

OPPOSITE, BOTTOM
Pashley benefits from mesmerizing views of the peaceful Sussex landscape. Sculptures appear throughout, but the end of a long vista, marking the transition from garden to countryside, is the perfect spot to place a focal point.

275

79

The Place for Plants

EAST BERGHOLT, SUFFOLK

The Place for Plants is more specifically a place for trees and shrubs. Originally laid out by Charles Eley between 1900 and 1914, the 6-hectare (15-acre) garden and arboretum are renowned for their rare trees, their collection of magnolias, camellias and rhododendrons, and the National Collection of deciduous *Euonymus*. Grass paths meander through eye-catching combinations of trees, such as *Ilex purpurea*, a holly with greenish-purple leaves when young, beside *Prunus* 'Royal Burgundy', a purple-leaved ornamental cherry, and *Elaeagnus angustifolia* 'Quicksilver', a fast-growing shrub with tapered, silver-scaled leaves. A stream cascades down steps from the top of the garden, ending in a still gully. Its borders are artfully planted with irises, candelabra primulas, hostas and rushes in a pleasing predominance of maroon, yellow and blue, while huge-leaved gunneras provide structure and shade. The path leads back through fine topiary to the walled garden, which is now a plant centre – hence the name of this garden.

RIGHT
Yew (*Taxus baccata*) is a very hardy, shade-tolerant, long-lived conifer, ideal for topiary.

OPPOSITE
Immaculately cut each autumn, these phenomenal yew spirals near the house rise out of giant sculpted blocks.

ABOVE
In autumn the mid-green leaves of
Liquidambar styraciflua turn glorious
orange, red and purple.

RIGHT
The stream sets a more tranquil
scene, where the sound of water as
well as the colours of the foliage
gladden the senses.

FAR RIGHT
Although the Place for Plants is
a joy in spring, with flowering
shrubs underplanted with bulbs,
it is equally arresting in autumn,
when so many of the trees are ablaze
with brilliant colour.

80

Kiftsgate Court

CHIPPING CAMPDEN, GLOUCESTERSHIRE

This remarkable garden, a paradise for plantspeople, was created from scratch by three generations of women. A dramatic set of terraces surrounding a stone house on a steep Cotswold escarpment, it is home to the famous Kiftsgate rose, and incorporates contemporary features with brilliant success. Spectacular Scots pines frame views of the Malvern Hills, while immediately below, a dark-blue half-moon pool glistens invitingly. A hedge of red–maroon *Berberis thunbergii* f. *atropurpurea* 'Rose Glow' at the entrance sets a colour theme that is repeated throughout in stupendous copper beeches and acers as well as roses and heucheras. A stimulating but harmonious variety of plants fills a series of different areas. At the end of the upper terrace, through a window cut in a yew hedge, one first glimpses a minimalist water garden. The rectangles of black water, white stone and turf, with slender poles holding bronze-leaved trickling water, are breathtaking.

RIGHT
Beyond *Lilium regale* stands the high portico of a Georgian façade. It was moved here from a house in Mickleton built by an ancestor of Sydney Graves Hamilton, who built Victorian Kiftsgate Court behind it.

OPPOSITE, TOP
This sunken garden with pool and wellhead fountain was originally designed to be white, but over the years colours have been introduced. In spring it is filled with bulbs.

OPPOSITE, BOTTOM LEFT
Paeonia lactiflora 'Immaculée'.

OPPOSITE, BOTTOM RIGHT
Within an enclosure of clipped yew is a surprise water garden. Height and movement are provided by a fountain of twenty-four bronze philodendron leaves on stems by Simon Allison.

OVERLEAF
The half-moon swimming pool was painted black more than a decade ago, to blend better with the stunning views of the Malvern Hills to the west. The surroundings glow like embers with the setting of the sun.

81

Somerset Lodge

PETWORTH, WEST SUSSEX

The charm of this 0.2-hectare (½-acre) garden lies in skilled attention to detail, especially in the hard landscaping, and in the obvious devotion lavished on it. Like a loved and happy child, it gives back warmth and delight. The fact that the owners, Mr and Mrs Harris, are architects is significant. When they moved here twenty years ago, the land was a sloping orchard on top of medieval streets. They dug out stone to make retaining walls, and moved earth to lessen the slope, although there is still a 5-metre (17-ft) drop from the highest to the lowest level. The overall design is based on diagonals. The house is in the corner of the plot, and the eye is drawn either to the gazebo or to the distant hills. Because the diagonal axis is longer, the length of the garden appears greater. Beautiful unseasoned oak, carved by Mr Harris, unifies the various areas: balustrading with chess-piece finials surrounds a formal lawn; even compost is housed in an elaborate oak 'compostela'.

RIGHT
Lilies and peonies frame a sundial, which leads the eye past a pond, an apple tree and a lawn to the seventeenth-century house.

OPPOSITE, TOP LEFT
The wooden gazebo with its lead roof was made by Mr Harris, and is based on the design of one at Trinity College, Cambridge.

OPPOSITE, TOP RIGHT
The gazebo plays an important role in the garden: one is always aware of being either above or below it.

OPPOSITE, BOTTOM LEFT
Curved box hedging makes a rhythmic parterre, perfectly setting off the herbs, vegetables and flowers within.

OPPOSITE, BOTTOM RIGHT
The centifolia rose 'Robert le Diable' under an apple tree.

OVERLEAF
Dawn light gilds the border and North Downs beyond. Among the old roses here are 'Königin von Dänemark', 'Marie Louise' and 'Comtesse du Cayla'.

82

The Old Barn

STONEY MIDDLETON, DERBYSHIRE

For its owners, Charles and Mary Richardson, the elevation of this garden – set 229 metres (750 ft) above sea level – with views of the Peak District on every side, gives it spirituality. It is also a place of great tranquillity and artistry in planting. When the Richardsons arrived in 1998 (with many more lorries of plants than of furniture), Mary started the garden from scratch, having always been a keen gardener and plantswoman: Charles says that 'gardening is like breathing to her'. A procession of hedged areas on a central axis protects against the wind, and incorporates a gazebo with roses, a chamomile lawn and an oak gate made by a craftsman who made one for Highgrove. Stepping down into a gorgeously planted D-shaped herbaceous border is like entering the stalls of a theatre, where box and yew could be the audience watching a tableau. But the garden becomes increasingly natural and relaxed, and, near the end, a plaque bears the inscription *Et in Arcadia nos* ('We too have lived in Arcadia').

RIGHT
From the house, the eye is drawn straight down aesthetically satisfying, uniform rooms, ending in open countryside.

OPPOSITE, TOP
The front parterre, harmonious and calm in its symmetry, was once a car park. The pink patio rose 'Queen Mother' is held in box.

OPPOSITE, BOTTOM
A wildlife pond is the habitat of crested newts, toads and frogs. In the foreground, variegated euonymus is planted by a seductive seat under a birch tree.

ABOVE
The kitchen garden is bordered by box, with honeysuckle and damson trees on the right and 'borrowed' views of the Peak District beyond.

RIGHT
Chives, onions, rhubarb, beans and lettuce form a geometric still life in the kitchen garden, in contrast with the untamed escarpment in the distance.

OPPOSITE, TOP
A lane was created here, separating horticulture from agriculture. On the left is a fabulous wild-flower meadow in summer; in spring, snowdrops and aconites grow there.

OPPOSITE, BOTTOM
A copse of silver birch beside a dry-stone wall: elegant simplicity.

83

Constable Burton Hall

LEYBURN, NORTH YORKSHIRE

After Charles Wyvill's father died when he was very young, Constable Burton Hall was temporarily leased to plantswoman Vida Burdon who, between 1933 and 1976, transformed the borders while keeping the backdrop of ancient yew trees. Charles has continued to enhance the garden, resurrecting two serene ponds from a neglected area. Other notable features are the woodland, with its carpets of naturalized bulbs, and the fabulous display of tulips in beds nearer the house. A few years ago Charles visited Keukenhof garden outside Amsterdam, and he was so impressed that he contacted Bloms Bulbs, which was seeking a northern garden to showcase its tulip bulbs. Every year the company gives Charles more than 6000 bulbs, which are planted mainly in blocks throughout the garden. One long, curved border is always planted with tulips of a single colour, a sensational sight.

RIGHT
Grass paths wind between beds of mixed tulips. A stone urn on a tall pillar adds height and drama.

OPPOSITE
The house was built for Sir Marmaduke Wyvill by John Carr in 1768. Its stone walls and surrounding handsome trees throw shadows on the lawn in evening light. In the foreground massed plantings of peony-flowered tulips dazzle.

OVERLEAF
A splendid avenue of mature beech trees provides dappled shade in May and glorious colour in autumn.

84

Linden Lodge

WILBERFOSS, EAST YORKSHIRE

Many of the features expected in a large
English country garden are to be found at
Linden Lodge, with its far-reaching views
of the Wolds, yet it is only nine years old
and 0.4 hectares (1 acre). Its owners, Robert
Scott (head gardener at York University) and
Jarrod Marsden, designed and created this
ambitious, many-faceted garden themselves.
Robert marked out the borders and paths,
and they rotavated old turf, felled some trees
and planted many indigenous ones. They
propagated herbaceous perennials, planted
borders, a small woodland area, an orchard
and a kitchen garden, and created a formal
pond, wildlife pond and bog garden. They
barrowed in about 30 tons of gravel to
make ribbon-like paths, bordered by box
or lavender. Jarrod and Robert maintain
the garden themselves, both having always
wanted a larger-than-average garden. They
hope not to move, but to stay and watch the
garden develop and mature — an ongoing,
evolving dream.

RIGHT
Robinia pseudoacacia 'Frisia' gracefully
frames a fountain and formal pond.

OPPOSITE, TOP
A bridge over the wildlife pond
leads towards the house, past mixed
plantings within well-defined box.

OPPOSITE, BOTTOM
A path meanders through
herbaceous planting towards striking
white agapanthus in a black urn,
with fragrant pink *Rosa* 'Gertrude
Jekyll' below, in a circle of *Lavandula
angustifolia* 'Hidcote'.

RIGHT

A cold frame holds agapanthus in the kitchen garden. A Gothic arch, designed by Robert, in a hedge in the orchard, allows views beyond.

OPPOSITE, TOP

Two golden privet hedges flank the herb and vegetable potager, embellished with a sundial on an ornate pillar. In the foreground is *Lavandula angustifolia* 'Munstead', while on the right, small terracotta pots on posts hold netting above brassicas.

OPPOSITE, BOTTOM

Yellow hemerocallis adds a touch of sparkle. Behind, in a curvaceous bed, the large-leaved tree *Catalpa bignonioides* partners *Photinia* ✕ *fraseri* 'Red Robin'.

85

Bonython Manor

CURY CROSS LANES, CORNWALL

Water, reflections and light play important roles in Bonython, on the Lizard Peninsula, England's southernmost point. A perfect grey doll's-house-style Georgian manor is mirrored in a still, oval pool. Each of the three manmade lakes in the extensive parkland reflects a different character: hot colour from exotic South African plants; tranquillity with shrubs and specimen trees; and ghostly green in the quarry lake, surrounded by cliffs, tree ferns and bamboo. Linking them are two streams edged with a haze of blue camassias. Colour, texture and movement are also integral to this diverse garden, most especially in the lavish herbaceous borders of the walled garden, and in the vibrant South African areas with their airy waves of ornamental grasses. It is extraordinary to think that this garden is the result of only ten years' work, largely that of South African-born Mrs Nathan, who lives here with her husband.

RIGHT, TOP
Elegant oak gates open into the potager.

RIGHT, BOTTOM
Achillea millefolium 'Cerise Queen' with white *A. millefolium.*

OPPOSITE
At the corner of the potager, planted with both vegetables and flowers, is a thatched propagating house.

Explosions of fiery colours around
this sheltered lake are reminiscent
of South Africa. Cannas, rudbeckias
and proteas take centre stage in
late summer, punctuated by the
billowing fronds of *Stipa arundinacea*,
which turns bronze in autumn.

BELOW, FROM TOP
Miscanthus sinensis; *Canna indica*
'Purpurea'.

OPPOSITE, TOP
Colour and texture excite in drifts of
grasses and plants that thrive in the
Cornish climate, set off by a dark
backcloth of established trees.

OPPOSITE, BOTTOM
Alliums add a sculptural touch to
the planting in the potager.

302

87

Great Thurlow Hall

HAVERHILL, SUFFOLK

This traditional English country garden
has not changed substantially over the last
forty years, and its 8 hectares (20 acres)
are maintained by gardeners. Its delights are
many: a trout river runs through it, and
there are abundant kitchen and rose gardens,
spacious lawns, old trees and fabulous
displays of bulbs in spring. The land is
pleasantly undulating, and there is a feeling
of openness and calm, with little sound
other than that of birds and water. A weir of
York stone has recently been put in, so when
one sits by one of the wooden bridges over
the river, there is a wonderful sound of
gushing water. The three sons of the house
love fishing in the river and in the lake,
which has an island in the middle, where
they can light campfires. It has been a
wonderful garden for them to grow up in.

RIGHT
Water is important in this garden.
A large lake reflects the house, a
willow tree and a tall beech hedge.

OPPOSITE, TOP
The back of the house (originally
Tudor) looks over a huge lawn, where
a copper beech is underplanted with
mixed narcissi.

OPPOSITE, BOTTOM
A gravel drive leading to the house is
thickly bordered in spring with some
of the 4 tons of narcissus bulbs
imported by the owner's grandfather.

ABOVE
At the back of the house, stepping-stones lead to the unusually shaped pond. Two spreading firs frame the distant landscape.

RIGHT
Four wooden bridges span the river, which is edged by narcissi and weeping willows.

OPPOSITE
The garden contains extensive shrubberies, woodland and an arboretum. Before the narcissi, the ground is white with snowdrops.

88

Cedar Farm

DESBOROUGH, NORTHAMPTONSHIRE

When the Tuffens moved to their family house in 1965, there was no garden there; instead, Mrs Tuffen ran a pig farm. She started to create the 4-hectare (10-acre) garden only in 1992, and yet there is an appearance of maturity as well as variety. This has partly been achieved because existing trees were kept, and different areas have evolved. A beautiful rose garden replaced the old muck heap, so that one is now completely enclosed by colour and perfume. Spectacular rampant roses were also planted to grow through plum trees retained in the orchard. As well as curving colour-themed borders, there are wide lawns, a wild area and ponds, since Mrs Tuffen likes space rather than 'garden rooms', and aimed to create her own dream, not a show garden. With her agricultural background, she is happiest outside: 'In my dotage I shall sit in the secret garden with my shawl, and no one will see me.' As I left Cedar Farm, her daughter, Zoe, gave me some beautiful iris plants from this generous garden.

RIGHT
The 'secret garden' is so-called because a sunken seat within cleverly enables one to look up into the faces of hellebores in winter and to be surrounded by roses in summer. *R.* 'Handel' climbs up the left of the pergola, 'Paul's Himalayan Musk' clothes the top, and at the gate is 'Compassion'.

OPPOSITE, TOP
The roof of the gazebo above the seat is clad in a mantle of 'Francis E. Lester' roses, which love the clay soil. Darker 'Gruss an Teplitz' is just visible behind; 'Compassion' is in the foreground.

OPPOSITE, BOTTOM
A keen flower arranger, Mrs Tuffen uses those talents in the garden, considering height, colour and texture. The pergola is a cloud of *R.* 'Paul's Himalayan Musk', and the dusky clematis is 'Proteus'.

89

Hillbark

BARDSEY, WEST YORKSHIRE

One might suppose that this 0.4-hectare (1-acre) garden was professionally designed and planted, yet it is the achievement of its two owners, Tim Gittins and Malcolm Simm, over the past twenty years. Their only help was in getting a technical plan drawn up from their design instructions, enabling contractors to build terraces on the sloping site and dig out a large pond. The garden is planted on three levels, each with its own particular quality, with more formal areas near the house at the top. Rhythmic evergreen structure and distinctive topiary combine with abundant perennials, as well as marginal planting around ponds and a stream. Tim and Malcolm were inspired by private gardens open for the National Gardens Scheme, to which they could relate, and are now proud to be part of the scheme themselves. For ten years they lived in the house next-door-but-one, and their fantasy was to create a fabulous garden out of the brambles and nettles: a dream come true.

RIGHT, TOP
The house is seen at the top of the garden, past a wooden bridge over the pond. Greens of all shades are key.

RIGHT, CENTRE
A gravel path weaves past irises, aquilegia and candelabra primulas by the stream. In the centre an ornamental piece of driftwood creates a focal point, while fastigiate yews add height and structure.

RIGHT, BOTTOM
Topiary provides winter interest throughout, most strikingly in the centre of the garden, where a sundial is surrounded by onion domes of clipped box. *Rosa* 'Sweet Juliet' is planted here, too, for its strong perfume in summer.

OPPOSITE
A fairly recent addition is a much-loved summer house, designed and built entirely from scratch by Malcolm as a retirement project. It is an ideal vantage point from which to plan further developments.

ABOVE
Sun glows through the willow by the
pond. A cardoon adds a grey–green
accent in the foreground.

RIGHT
Serpentine stone steps lead from
the top to the middle level. The pot,
made by Malcolm, holds echeveria;
scented *Phuopsis stylosa* is on the other
side of the path.

FAR RIGHT
This large pond, created by the
owners around one existing weeping
willow, is now an area of tranquillity.

90

Cressing Temple

BRAINTREE, ESSEX

In 1137 Cressing Temple was granted by Queen Matilda to the Knights Templar. Today, two vast Templar barns are the only original buildings that remain. There is, however, a tranquil walled garden, originally built in Tudor times and redesigned and planted in 1994. Inside, faded herringbone brick paths lead to several areas: a forecourt planted with strewing herbs; a reconstructed Elizabethan knot garden; a nosegay garden with scented plants; medicinal, dyer's and culinary borders (the latter with an astounding number of mint varieties); an orchard; a vegetable garden; a flowery mead; and an arbour or walkway covered with hops and eglantine rose. All the plants used were available in late medieval and Tudor times. The central feature is a brick fountain with four spouts symbolizing the rivers of Paradise. Colours are subdued and soft – greys, mauves and greens – and are complemented by the sounds of running water and humming bees. Precise, geometric, clipped hedges provide a sense of order and calm, while mounds of cotton lavender (*Santolina chamaecyparissus*) add an element of relaxed comfort.

The knot garden is enclosed by a hawthorn hedge, with a central brick fountain and a rill running towards the barley barn. The building on the right was for wheat. Both barns have peg-tiled roofs, harmonizing with the brick paving. The knots are dexterously interwoven patterns of different plants. Here are short box and grey santolina, with taller wall germander (*Teucrium chamaedrys*) in the centre. The outer sections are, unusually, filled with white shells; others have pebbles, earth and gravel.

316

91

Seend Manor

DEVIZES, WILTSHIRE

Visiting Seend Manor is like going on a magical journey through different countries. Seemingly, no expense has been spared to provide authentic, tasteful detail in this unique garden, designed by its owners, Amanda and Stephen Clark, in collaboration with Julian and Isabel Bannerman (of Highgrove fame). The garden tells the story of the Clarks' lives. A nostalgic English garden is filled with perfumed roses and herbaceous plants. Within a tall yew hedge is an elegant African garden (Stephen was born in South Africa), where a geometric, raised lily pond holds a central stone obelisk surrounded by four sphinxes. The circular Chinese garden (Amanda's parents lived in Hong Kong and China) incorporates a pebbled floor, painstakingly copied from a Suzhou design; a large, red-painted wooden pavilion; and stone lions saved from a Chinese village that was being demolished. Bamboo, peonies and tree ferns emerge from genuine Chinese rocks.

RIGHT, TOP
Teak obelisks and arches made in Thailand support pale-pink *Rosa* 'Félicité Perpétue' and creamy 'Adélaïde d'Orléans'.

RIGHT, CENTRE
The garden is quartered by pleached hornbeam *allées* leading from a central fountain. The green-oak temple and throne were designed by the Bannermans; the seat bears a Latin inscription roughly meaning 'Please keep off my chair'.

RIGHT, BOTTOM
The heated swimming pool is flanked by cylindrically cut *Quercus ilex*. The doors in the loggia lead to a kitchen and a shower room.

OPPOSITE, TOP
The English garden gifts colour and scent: roses, lavender, delphiniums, lilies and peonies within box. The central pergola is festooned with *Rosa* 'Awakening', with 'New Dawn' below.

OPPOSITE, BOTTOM
An Italian stone fountain is surrounded by ivy trained by Stephen on wires to form a pattern.

93

The Old Rectory

NETHERBURY, DORSET

Keen plantsmanship combines with deft overall planning in this ravishing garden owned, designed and maintained by Amanda and Simon Mehigan. Admitting that they are 'not herbaceous-border people', they lovingly source rare species and plant them with increasing informality the further they are from the house, bearing in mind the relationships both within the garden and with the landscape. Since the Arts and Crafts movement, many gardeners claim to use informal planting within a strong framework, but plants frequently include delphiniums, roses, lavender and the like. Here, even in the courtyard garden, with box parterres and topiary, subtle flowers unusually include nigella, campanula, honesty, mallow and species tulips. Further from the house are a pond, a bog garden and an orchard with treasured snowdrops, fritillaries, wild orchids, camassia and *Paeonia emodi*. A seat in a beech 'house' at the end of the garden affords views down a central axis to Warren Hill. A castellated yew hedge mimics the adjacent church, and pyramid yews echo the house gables; harmony is achieved throughout.

RIGHT
The bog garden is planted with large drifts of irises, *Anemone rivularis*, *Hosta sieboldiana* var. *elegans*, darker *H.* 'Blue Angel' and white arum lilies, revelling in the moist conditions.

PAGE 324, FROM TOP
At the front of the house, quirky box hedging holds lollipop hollies underplanted with species tulips; a mown path through grass strewn with buttercups and ox-eye daisies leads to a seat under a walnut tree.

PAGE 325
A series of enclosed gardens with a central *allée* gives a sense of ordered serenity. Beyond the courtyard, with its box-edged beds, the axis continues under rose arches bisected by beds of *Iris pallida*, towards clipped yews and fastigiate hornbeams. The path changes from herringbone brick to patterned cobbles to mown grass, varying the rhythm.

94

Wyken Hall
STANTON, SUFFOLK

This Elizabethan house is lime-washed
terracotta red, with grey-painted window
frames and brick chimneys. Paths in the
formal gardens wrapped around the hall
are of patterned brick; seats, arches and
gates are painted blue, giving unity to this
multifaceted garden designed over the last
twenty-five years. Blessed by an existing
structure of flint walls and fine old trees, the
owner, Sir Kenneth Carlisle, established an
old-fashioned rose garden, with a pergola
replicating in miniature one in the garden
at Bodnant in Wales, where he spent his
childhood. When Kenneth married, in 1986,
his wife, Carla, developed the gardens further,
and a knot and herb garden were designed
by Arabella Lennox-Boyd. The gardens
also now include a wild-flower meadow, a
copper beech maze, a woodland garden and
a vineyard. Throughout the formal parts of
the garden, gaps in enclosures deliberately
reveal views of the countryside beyond,
while sculpted and real hares and sheep
coexist. The impression is one of scenes
and sets, and a beguiling whole.

RIGHT
This simple herb garden was designed
by Arabella Lennox-Boyd during a
weekend visit in 1983. Surrounding
the sundial are oregano and chives.
Above low box hedging, the house
walls are clothed with pink *Solanum
jasminoides*, yellow *Fremontodendron
californicum* and *Wisteria sinensis*.

OPPOSITE, TOP
A fountain adds movement, sound
and light to a brick pathway between
double mixed borders.

OPPOSITE, BOTTOM
'Spartan' apples are espaliered so
as not to block the view from the
house. They are underplanted with
lavender for scent, and to match five
blue rocking chairs brought from
Carla's native Mississippi, to remind
her of a Southern veranda.

OPPOSITE, TOP
A Japanese-inspired garden glows with the colours of backlit maples.

OPPOSITE, BOTTOM LEFT
A sinuous seat contours the wildlife pond.

OPPOSITE, BOTTOM RIGHT
A charming bird house stands beside pampas grass, with the dramatic cedar silhouetted behind.

LEFT
Late-summer foliage is echoed by the ruby stained glass of the pavilion.

BELOW
Whimsical details add to a feeling of homeliness.

96

The Manor House

STEVINGTON, BEDFORDSHIRE

Imaginative and inspired, Stevington Manor garden is owned and designed by Kathy and Simon Brown. There are cottage, formal, winter and edible borders and exquisite colour combinations, and the use of grasses – whether feathery, furry, veil-like or, ignited by the sun, like sparklers – is memorable. Kathy's fascination with art has led her to re-create the essence and spirit of certain pictures in the garden. Her interest is in the emotional responses that plants provoke, and the effects of season, wind and, especially, light. A Mondrian-style wall, painted by son Jonathan, sparked five more conceptual gardens. The Hokusai garden envelops you in waves of miscanthus. A black-and-maroon Rothko room (with berberis, prunus and beech) is contemplative and sombre. In the Hepworth-inspired garden, planting of grasses, sedums and echinacea is not dense; space between, covered in green slate, is equally important. Grasses buffeted by the wind capture a moment in the Monet garden. In Kandinsky, colours in containers clash chaotically. The garden is the medium of Kathy's artistic expression.

RIGHT, TOP
A fan of pampas grass is seen with upright calamagrostis.

RIGHT, BOTTOM
Low sun shines on the gazebo, framed by silhouetted arches deliberately spaced to allow gaps of sky between.

OPPOSITE, TOP
Green bamboo appears either side of mixed miscanthus, of different heights, in the Hokusai border.

OPPOSITE, BOTTOM
Glowing, silky seed heads of *Clematis* 'Aureolin' form a web through which the gazebo is seen.

OVERLEAF
The elegant French garden, designed by Simon, commemorates the trial of Nicolas Fouquet in the early 1660s, with twelve yew jurors behind box parterres. Simon, a judge, cuts the topiary.

A statue of Leda and the Swan by
Enzo Plazzotta is silhouetted in
the bronze rays of the morning sun,
illuminating naturalized primulas
and narcissi on the far banks of
the Mermaid Pond.

98

Lavenham Priory

SUFFOLK

Gill and Tim Pitt have lived in this remarkable
lime-washed thirteenth-century building for
fifteen years, running a bed-and-breakfast.
They were lucky enough to inherit the
1.4-hectare (3½-acre) garden, which included
the atmospheric herb garden now maintained
by Gill. It contains virtually every herb for
culinary, medicinal and aromatic use as well
as for dyes (the wool trade was important to
Lavenham), arranged around a five-pointed
star of local flint. Here, scent combines with
the tones of silver and mauve and a sense of
history to create a secluded calm. The rest
of the garden, mainly tended by Tim, opens
up to include a vegetable patch; a long lawn;
a large spring-fed pond (originally used
for livestock and reclaimed by removing
2500 tons of builders' rubble); an orchard
of walnuts, plums, local apples and pears;
and many English species of tree and hedge.
Tim planted many of the trees himself,
and cuts all the hedges. He advises: 'Get
the boundaries sorted, like a picture frame.
The rest flows from that.'

A stone sundial is surrounded by the
flint De Vere star. Alberic de Vere is
mentioned in the Domesday survey
of 1086 as being Lord of the manor
of Lavenham, and he allocated part
of his lands to the Canons for their
priory. The L-shaped building forms
two sides of the herb garden. The
central, cobbled star is set in a thyme
lawn; purple sage contributes depth of
colour on the left, with delicate grey
santolina at the back on the right.

LEFT
The serene millpond is seen from the
terrace. At the back, a scooped yew
hedge is a foil for the white flowers
of *Amelanchier lamarckii*. To the left,
an arbour of ivy, honeysuckle and
roses surrounds a bench with views
of urns filled with hyacinths, and
a leaping cat sculpted by Stephen
Charlton. Following the curve of
the lawn is cottage-loaf box topiary,
underplanted with *Tulipa* 'Queen
of Night'. In the foreground, box
rounds in tubs are backed by paler,
twiggy cotoneaster.

ABOVE
Narcissus 'Bridal Crown'.

349

Gardens Open to the Public

For information on National Gardens Scheme (NGS) gardens, see ngs.org.uk.
Gardens not listed below are not open to visitors at any time.

2 Garsington Manor, 28 Southend, Garsington, Oxon. OX44 9DH. Private; open for NGS and for the opera season. GarsingtonOpera.org.

6 Painswick Rococo Garden, Painswick, Glos. GL6 6TH. Jan–Oct. www.RococoGarden.org.uk.

7 The Kitchen Garden, Church Cottage, Church Lane, Troston, Suffolk IP31 1EX. Easter–Sept: Fri and Sat. Also for NGS and for hen-keeping courses. Kitchen-garden-hens.co.uk.

8 NGS only. Shdcottages.co.uk.

9 Hatfield House, Hatfield, Herts. AL9 5NQ. Apr–Sept: Weds–Sun; daily in Jul and Aug. Hatfield-house.co.uk.

10 NGS only.

11 NGS only.

12 NGS only.

13 Petworth, W. Sussex GU28 0AE. Mar–Nov: Sat–Weds. NationalTrust.org.uk.

14 The Old Rectory, Sudborough, Northants. NN14 3BX. Mar–Sept. OldRectoryGardens.co.uk.

16 Chenies Manor, Chenies, Bucks. WD3 6ER. Weds, Thurs and Bank Holiday Mon 2–5 pm. CheniesManorHouse.co.uk.

17 Lamorran House Gardens, Upper Castle Road, St Mawes, Cornwall TR2 5BZ. Apr–Sept. LamorranGardens.co.uk.

18 Inner Temple, London EC4Y 7HL. Weekdays 12.30–3 pm. www.InnerTemple.org.uk.

23 Sissinghurst Castle, near Cranbrook, Kent TN17 2AB. Mar–Nov: Fri–Tues. NationalTrust.org.uk.

24 Blakenham Woodland Garden, Little Blakenham, Ipswich, Suffolk IP8 4LZ. Mar–Jul. www.Blakenham WoodlandGarden.org.uk.

25 NGS only.

27 Helmingham Hall, Stowmarket, Suffolk IP14 6EF. May and Sept: Sun and Weds pm; Jun–Aug: Tues–Thurs, Sun pm and Bank Holiday Mon. Helmingham.com.

28 NGS only.

29 NGS only.

30 NGS only.

31 Hestercombe, Cheddon Fitzpaine, Taunton, Somerset TA2 8LG. Daily. Hestercombe.com.

33 NGS only. TilfordCottageGarden.co.uk.

34 Easton Lodge, Little Easton, Great Dunmow, Essex CM6 2BB. Closed, but may reopen; see EastonLodge.co.uk.

35 The Beth Chatto Gardens, Elmstead Market, Colchester, Essex CO7 7DB. Feb–Nov. BethChatto.co.uk.

36 The Lucy Redman School of Garden Design, 6 The Village, Rushbrooke, Bury St Edmunds, Suffolk IP30 0ER. Easter – end Sept: Fri; also by appointment and for NGS. See LucyRedman.co.uk for dates and courses.

37 Broughton Castle, near Banbury, Oxon. OX15 5EB. May–Sept: Weds, Sun and Bank Holiday Mon 2–5 pm; also Thurs in Jul and Aug. BroughtonCastle.com.

38 Marks Hall, Coggeshall, Essex CO6 1TG. Apr–Oct: Tues–Sun and Bank Holiday Mon. MarksHall.org.uk.

42 Gravetye Manor, Vowels Lane, East Grinstead, W. Sussex RH19 4LJ. Private; open to hotel guests and diners. GravetyeManor.co.uk.

43 Lady Farm, Chelwood, Somerset BS39 4NN. Jun–Oct: first Sun in the month (pm). LadyFarm.com.

45 Cholmondeley Castle, Malpas, Cheshire SY14 8AH. Apr–Sept: Weds, Thurs, Sun and Bank Holiday Mon. CholmondeleyCastle.com.

48 Walsingham Abbey, Walsingham, Norfolk. Feb–Oct. WalsinghamAnglican.org.uk/ information/tourist_information.htm.

49 NGS only.

50 Rousham, Oxon. OX25 4QU. Daily. Rousham.org.

51 Colesbourne Park, Colesbourne, Cheltenham, Glos. GL53 9NP. Specific days for snowdrops and other spring bulbs; see snowdrop.org.uk.

52 NGS only.

54 NGS only.

55 Chiffchaffs, Chaffeymoor, Bourton, Gillingham, Dorset SP8 5AY. Mar–Sept: Weds, Thurs, and first and third Sun pm.

56 28 Kensington Road, Bristol BS5 7NB. Private; open by appointment and for NGS. victorianhousegarden.pwp. blueyonder.co.uk.

59 David Austin Roses, Bowling Green Lane, Albrighton, Wolverhampton, W. Midlands WV7 3HB. Daily. DavidAustinRoses.com.

60 Buscot Park, Faringdon, Oxon. SN7 8BU. Apr–Sept: Mon–Fri and some Sat and Sun. Buscot-park.com

61 Abbotsbury Subtropical Gardens, Bullers Way, Abbotsbury, Dorset DT3 4LA. Daily. Abbotsbury-tourism.co.uk/gardens.

64 Haddon Lake House, St Lawrence, Isle of Wight PO38 1XR. Private; open by appointment. LakeHouseDesign.co.uk.

65 Ripley Castle, Harrogate, N. Yorks HG3 3AY. Daily. www.RipleyCastle.co.uk.

66 Hever Castle, Edenbridge, Kent TN8 7NG. Mar: Weds–Sun; Apr–Oct: daily; Nov–Dec: Thurs–Sun. HeverCastle.co.uk.

67 Trebah Garden, Mawnan Smith, Falmouth, Cornwall TR11 5JZ. Daily. TrebahGarden.co.uk.

68 Barnards Farm, Brentwood Road, West Horndon, Essex CM13 3LX. Apr–Aug: Thurs. Also for NGS. BarnardsFarm.eu.

69 Goodnestone Park, Wingham, Kent CT3 1PL. Mar–Oct: Tues–Fri, Sun and Bank Holiday Mon. GoodnestoneParkGardens.co.uk.

70 The Exotic Garden, 126 Thorpe Road, Norwich, Norfolk NR1 1UL. Jun–Oct: Sun pm. ExoticGarden.com.

71 Gibberd Garden, Marsh Lane, Gilden Way, Harlow, Essex CM17 0NA. Apr–Sept: Weds, Sat, Sun and Bank Holiday pm. TheGibberdGarden.co.uk.

72 Smallwood Farmhouse, Bradfield St George, Bury St Edmunds, Suffolk IP30 0AJ. Private; open by appointment through *The Good Gardens Guide*.

73 Renishaw Hall, Sheffield S1 3WB. Apr–Sept: Thurs–Sun. Sitwell.co.uk.

74 NGS only.

75 Hodsock Priory, Blythe, Worksop, Notts. SBI 0TY. Feb. HodsockPriory.com.

76 Saling Hall, Great Saling, Braintree, Essex CM7 5DT. Open for NGS May–Jul: Weds pm. SalingHall.com.

77 NGS only.

78 Pashley Manor, Ticehurst, near Wadhurst, E. Sussex TN5 7HE. Apr–Sept. PashleyManorGardens.com.

79 The Place for Plants, East Bergholt Place, Suffolk CO7 6UP. Daily. PlaceForPlants.co.uk.

80 Kiftsgate Court, Chipping Campden, Glos. GL55 6LN. Apr–Sept: varying days; see kiftsgate.co.uk.

83 Constable Burton Hall, Leyburn, N. Yorks DL8 5LJ. Mar–Sept. www.ConstableBurtonGardens.co.uk.

84 NGS only.

85 Bonython Manor, Cury Cross Lanes, Helston, Cornwall TR12 7BA. Apr–Sept: Mon–Fri.

87 NGS only.

88 NGS only.

89 NGS only.

90 Cressing Temple, Witham Road, Cressing, Braintree, Essex CM77 8PD. Mar–Oct: daily except Sat. CressingTemple.org.uk.

91 Seend Manor, Seend, near Melksham, Devizes, Wilts. SN12 6NT. By appointment only. 01380 828422.

93 NGS only.

94 Wyken Hall, Stanton, near Bury St Edmunds, Suffolk IP31 2DW. Apr–Sept: Sun–Fri pm. WykenVineyards.co.uk/gardens.php.

95 Marle Place, Brenchley, Tonbridge, Kent TN12 7HS. Apr–Oct. MarlePlace.co.uk.

96 The Manor House, Church Road, Stevington, Beds. MK43 7QB. Private; open on specific days (see KathyBrownsGarden.homestead.com), for NGS and by appointment.

97 Forde Abbey, Chard, Somerset TA20 4LU. Daily. FordeAbbey.co.uk.

99 Hole Park, Rolvenden, Cranbrook, Kent. Mar–Oct: Weds and Thurs; some Sun and Bank Holiday Mon; daily in spring. HolePark.com.

100 Mill Dene, School Lane, Blockley, Moreton-in-Marsh, Glos. GL56 9HU. Apr–Sept: Tues–Fri and some weekends; see MillDeneGarden.co.uk.

Index

AUTHOR'S ACKNOWLEDGEMENTS

For this book more than any other, I owe thanks to my husband, Robin. He spent countless weekends driving me all round England to visit gardens, cancelled a holiday and offered constant support; I could not have written the book without him. It has been a privilege and pleasure to work with Jerry and Marcus Harpur, whose photos make this book. I also thank Claire Bent-Marshall at Harpur Garden Images for her help. I am grateful to many friends for encouragement and forbearance, in particular Christine Thomas, Davina McTiernan and Marjorie Sweetko. Finally, special thanks to Claire Chandler at Merrell for commissioning me to write the book, and to Rosanna Lewis, project editor, who was a joy to work with.

PHOTOGRAPHERS' ACKNOWLEDGEMENTS

We are grateful to all the garden owners and designers involved in the creation of the hundred gardens in this book. Without them it would not have been such an enormous pleasure to have produced the photographs herein: thank you all.

First published 2010 by

Merrell Publishers Limited
81 Southwark Street
London SE1 0HX

merrellpublishers.com

Text copyright © 2010 Barbara Baker
Illustrations copyright © 2010 Jerry Harpur, except those on pages 2, 9, 28–31, 32t, 33–37, 44–45, 55b, 63tl, tr, bl, br, 74–77, 79b, 104–109, 118–24, 126br, 127–35, 146–49, 155–57, 162–71, 184–85, 190–93, 197b, 198tl, bl, 208, 209t, 216, 220–23, 240–45, 250–51, 252l, br, 254–55, 269b, 270bl, mr, br, 271, 306–309, 316–17, 326, 328–31, 337b, 338–45: © 2010 Marcus Harpur
Design and layout copyright © 2010 Merrell Publishers Limited

British Library Cataloguing-in-Publication data:
Baker, Barbara, 1952 Sept. 9 –
Dream gardens of England : 100 inspirational gardens.
1. Gardens – England – Pictorial works. 2. Gardens –
Design – Pictorial works.
I. Title II. Harpur, Jerry. III. Harpur, Marcus.
712.6'0942-dc22

ISBN 978-1-8589-4511-8

Produced by Merrell Publishers Limited
Designed by Jonny Burch
Project-managed by Rosanna Lewis

Printed and bound in China

JACKET, FRONT: Sleightholmedale Lodge, North Yorkshire (8)

JACKET, BACK (from top): Forde Abbey, Somerset (97); Sheephouse, Gloucestershire (57); Cholmondeley Castle, Cheshire (45)

FRONTISPIECE: Eastgrove Cottage, Worcestershire (5)

PAGE 4: Hatfield House, Hertfordshire (9)